Wildflowers

of

Chebeague

and the

Casco Bay Islands

George Bates

North
Country
Press

ISBN 978-1-943424-64-1

LCCN 2020951188

North Country Press
Unity, Maine

Table of Contents

INTRODUCTION

The focus of this book is the flowers found growing in the woods, fields, roadsides, and beaches of the islands of Casco Bay, Maine. Because my summer home is on Chebeague Island, most of the species recorded here were observed on Chebeague, and most specific place names refer to Chebeague. However, the flora of the islands of Casco Bay (and surrounding mainland) is all very similar; so, this book can be a guide to the wildflowers of the region. I wrote these pages primarily for myself, because I wanted to learn the wildflowers on Chebeague, but I also want to share them with anyone who may enjoy these plants. The species included here are mostly wildflowers although there are some quirky ones, like sheep sorrel (a horrible garden weed) and bittersweet (our worst invasive). Some may not consider these flowers; but of course they are, they're flowering plants. There are also some species here that are probably escaped ornamentals (e.g. foxglove and meadow pink), and so are not strictly "wild" flowers, but they are certainly pretty and worth including.

The flowers are arranged by month and within each month by color. The monthly arrangement gives a sense of the progression of the seasons from spring through fall. The arrangement by color is to help with identification. Designating a species to a particular month is somewhat arbitrary (should a flower first seen on May 31 be included in May or June?) and, depending on the weather in a given year, flowering times can be shifted by a week or more. Many species flower over several months (dandelions, clovers and hawkweeds, for example), but all of them have a period where flowering is most intense and this is where I have placed them. Arranging plants by flower color also has difficulties because some of the color distinctions are blurry – is a flower purple or is it more red or blue? I have grouped together red with pink and purple with blue.

For each plant I have included a description and, where I know them, details about their edibility/toxicity and uses. Many wildflowers have several common names. I have listed the most consistently used name first, followed, for some plants, by additional names. The scientific names are unambiguous but sometimes change as new information is learned about a species or genus. For example, about ten years ago, all the asters in the New World were moved from the genus *Aster* to new genera based on DNA sequence comparisons between New World and Old World asters.

Please remember that nearly all the land on the islands is either private property or in conservation easements. Observing the wildflowers is great; picking them without permission is not.

Please Don't Pick The Wildflowers!

Finally, I thank my son Luke who spent many hours with me entering and formatting the text and photos; his help was invaluable. Also, many thanks to my wife Carolyn Schultz and our friend Dana Bryan for help in proof reading and editing this book.

About the Author

George Bates is Professor Emeritus of Biological Science, Florida State University, where he conducted research on plant genetics and taught genetics, molecular biology, and plant biology. George has a life-long passion for the outdoors, nature, and plants — and for Chebeague and Casco Bay. Members of George's family have been Chebeaguers since the early 1800s; first as year-round islanders, later as summer residents. George and his wife Carolyn spend winters in Tallahassee, Florida, and summers on Chebeague Island, where they enjoy gardening, hiking, and boating on the bay. You can reach George by email at:
bates@bio.fsu.edu

May is a beautiful month for wildflowers.   This is when many of the understory plants in the woods flower and flowering begins at the forest edges and in our lawns.

Wild Lily-Of-The-Valley or Canada Mayflower
Maianthemum canadense

Family: ASPARAGACEAE

This plant is small, only 4 to 10 inches tall with 1 to 3 leaves per stem; the leaves are up to 3 inches long. Each individual flower has 4 tiny white petals and 4 stamens. Wild lily-of-the-valley is very common in the woods and at the edges of woods. It can form large stands, reproducing vegetatively by underground stems (rhizomes). Its berries are green at first, turning red as they ripen.

May-White

Wild Sarsaparilla
Aralia nudicaulis

Family: ARALIACEAE

Wild sarsaparilla is up to 2 feet tall; each stem divides into three leaves, with each leaf divided into 5 or 7 leaflets (pinnately compound leaves). Its flowers are formed on a separate stalk from the leaves, which also divides into three clusters of tiny white flowers with very small petals. This plant is a perennial, found in our woods often in large stands. Like wild lily-of-the-valley, it reproduces vegetatively by underground stems (rhizomes), as well as by seeds.

The roots of wild sarsaparilla have been used to make root beer and were used by some Native Americans to make tea.

Northern White Violet
Viola pallens

Family: VIOLACEAE

This white-flowered violet is a perennial found in moist woodland environments, lawns, and roadside ditches. The heart-shaped leaves are up to 2 inches long and 3 inches wide. I love the blue/purple streaks on the petals.

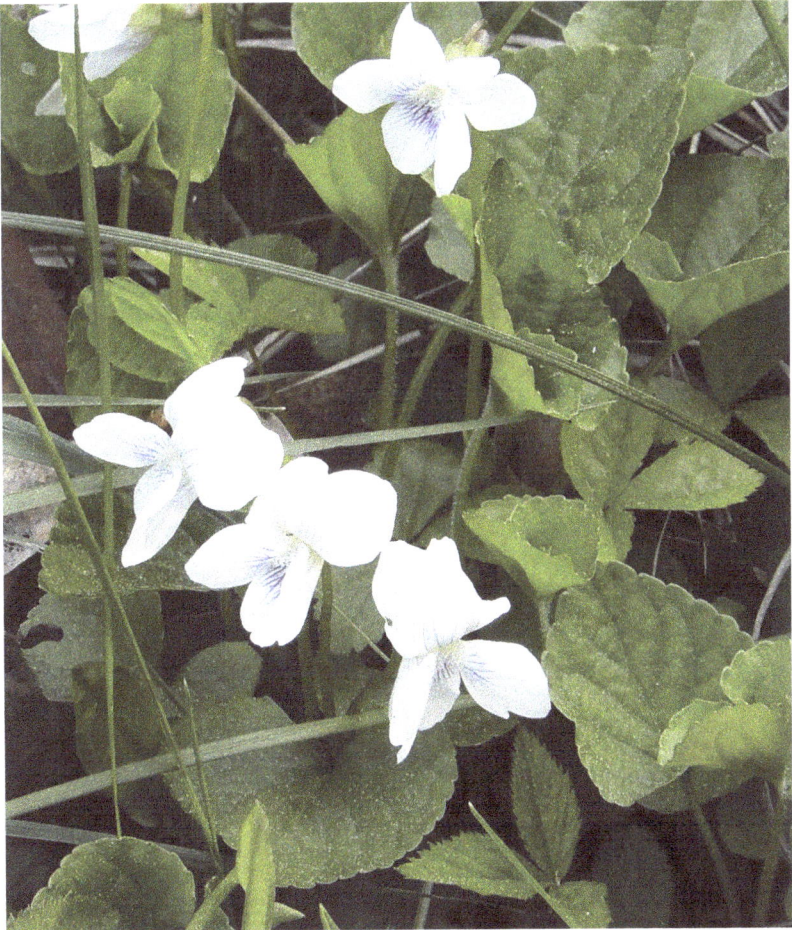

May-White

White Baneberry
Actaea pachypoda

Family: RANUNCULACEAE

Found in wooded but well-lit environments, white baneberry is 2 to 3 feet tall. The flowers are formed in a 2- to 3-inch-long cluster at the end of a long stalk. Individual flowers are about 1/8 inch across with prominent stamens and small white petals. The leaves are divided into multiple leaflets that are 2 to 4 inches long, broadly arrowhead-shaped, and sharply toothed.

The white berries this plant forms are toxic to humans, hence the name baneberry.

Wood Anemone
Anemone quinquefolia

Family: RANUNCULACEAE

This beautiful plant grows on the edge of wooded areas and is 6 to 12 inches tall, with a single white flower about 1 to 1½ inches across. The flower has 5 petals and lots of stamens. Each plant has two or three leaves that are divided into five (sometimes as few as three) leaflets that are 1 to 1½ inches long and have toothed margins.

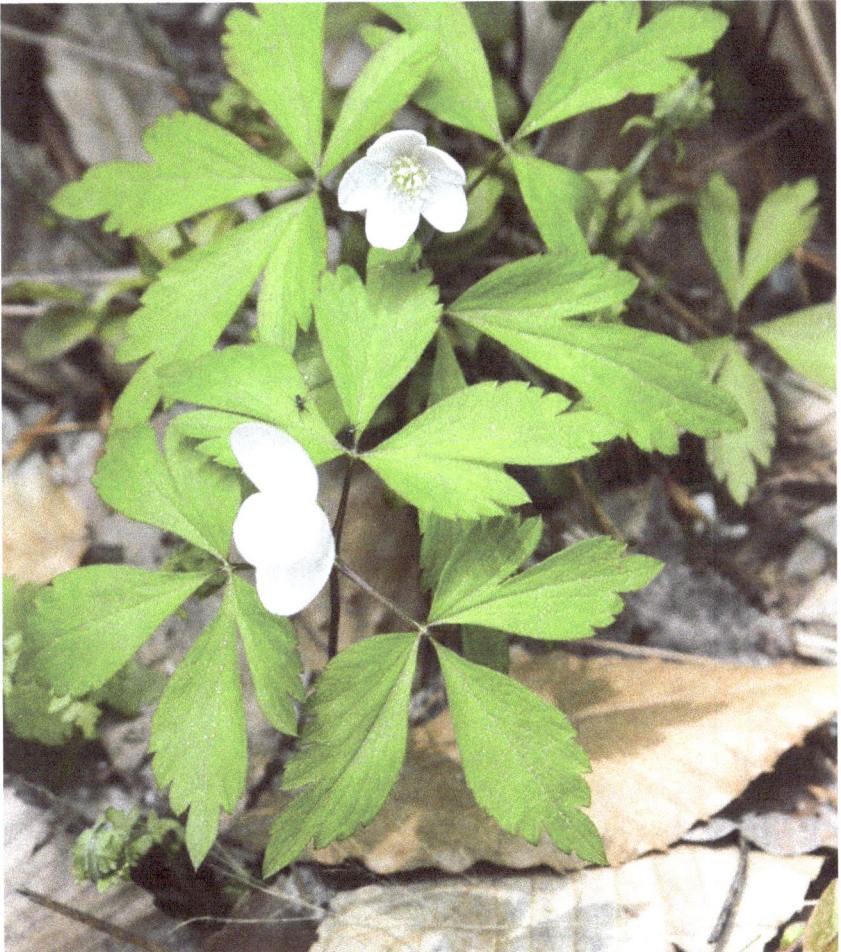

May-White

Starflower
Lysimachia borealis

Family: MYRSINACEAE

This woodland perennial can be up to 6 to 7 inches tall, with a single stalk, and a whorl of leaves 2 to 4 inches long. A pair of white flowers (sometimes only a single flower) forms in early spring. Along with wild sarsaparilla and wild lily-of-the-valley, this plant is very common in the understory of our spruce woods.

Bunchberry, Dwarf Dogwood
Chamaepericlymenum canadense (formerly *Cornus canadensis*)

Family: CORNACEAE

One of my favorites, this perennial is found at woodland edges and often occurs in large stands. It is about 6 inches tall with a single stalk, and a whorl of 4 to 6 leaves that are 2 to 3 inches long. The true flowers on this plant are small and greenish/tan, but they are surrounded by four, white, petal-like leaves (bracts). It forms red berries in late July to August.

Dwarf dogwood used to be classified in the genus *Cornus*, but all the other members of that genus are trees or shrubs and dwarf dogwood has been placed in a separate genus (*Chamaepericlymenum*).

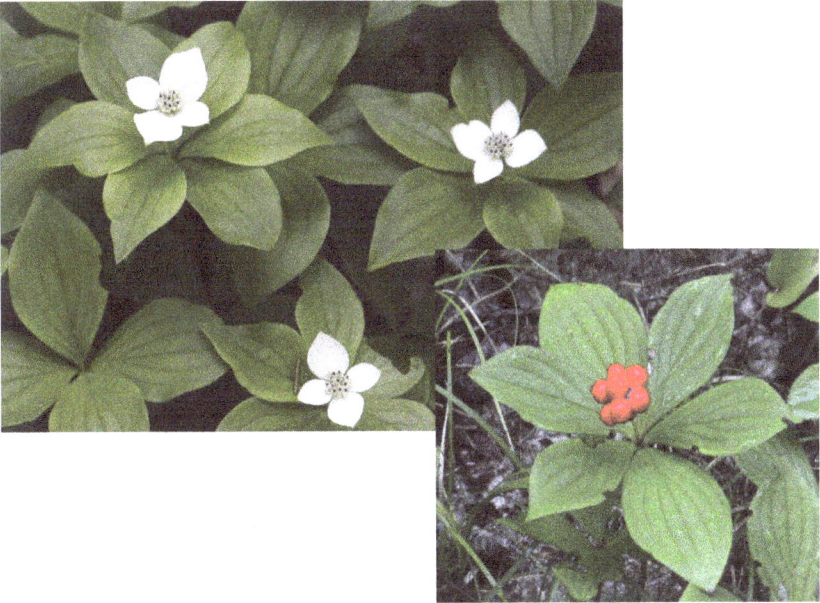

May-White

Hobblebush
Viburnum lantanoides

Family: ADOXACEAE

This woodland shrub is 10 to 12 feet high, and forms clusters of flowers, with white petals, in early spring. The leaves are 4 to 6 inches long, heart-shaped, and have finely toothed margins. The flower clusters are about 4 inches across. Hobblebush is sometimes called moosewood but we have another plant also called moosewood – *Acer pensylvanicum.*

Field Pussytoes
Antennaria neglecta

Family: ASTERACEAE

A perennial found in fields and on ledges. Field pussytoes has a basal rosette of lance-shaped leaves about 1 inch long, and a single flower stalk, 8 to 10 inches high, which ends in several clusters of tiny white flowers.

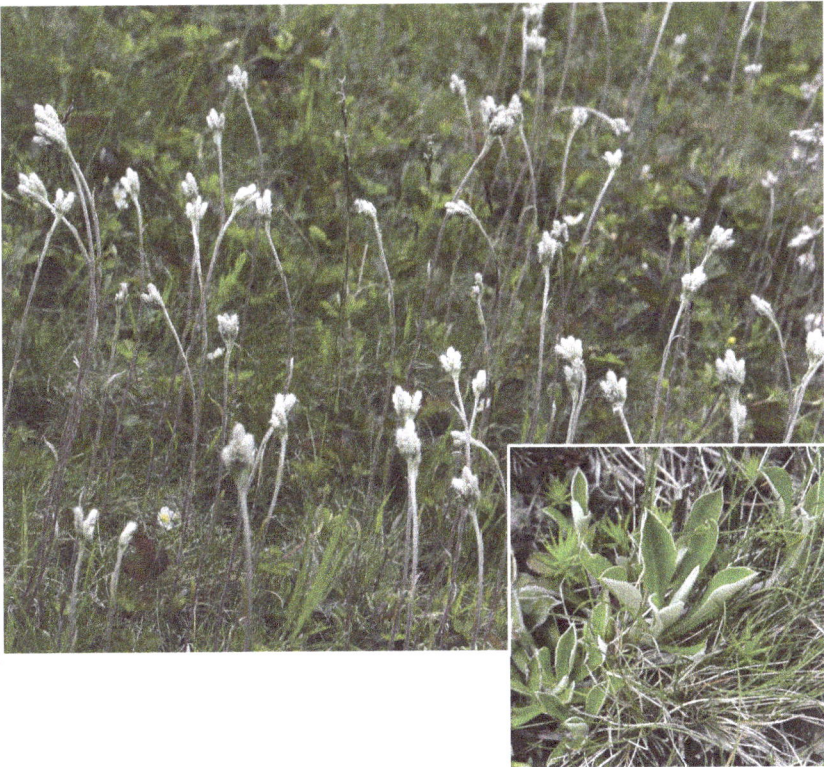

May-White

Wild Strawberry
Fragaria virginiana

Family: ROSACEAE

Wild strawberry is a perennial found in fields and lawns. It is up to 6 inches tall, with flowers (½ to 1 inch across) formed singly or in small clusters. Each leaf is divided into three leaflets that are strongly toothed (serrated). The terminal tooth on the central leaflet is shorter than the teeth below it, which distinguishes wild strawberry from the woodland strawberry (*Fragaria vesca*). And, of course, the fruits are yummy!

High Bush Blueberry
Vaccinium corymbosum

Family: ERICACEAE

A shrub 5 to 10 feet tall often found at woodland edges and swampy areas. We have several species of blueberries and huckleberries, and I
haven't sorted them out yet. Low bush blueberry is *Vaccinium angustifolium*. They all flower in early spring.

Highbush

Lowbush

May-White

Wild Calla Lily
Calla palustris

Family: ARACEAE

Found in bogs and swampy areas, wild calla lily is in the arum family along with jack-in-the-pulpit and skunk cabbage. The plant is 6 to 12 inches tall with heart-shaped leaves 2 to 4 inches long. All members of the arum family have their flowers organized in a characteristic structure called a spathe and spadix. The spadix is a spike that bears the actual individual flowers, and it is subtended, and partially surrounded, by a petal-like leaf, the spathe.

Spadix

Spathe

Solomon's Seal, Smooth Solomon's Seal
Polygonatum biflorum

Family: ASPARAGACEAE

Up to 3 feet tall, this easily identifiable perennial has clusters of 2 to 5, one-inch-long, tubular flowers that dangle from the base of each leaf. The leaves are broadly lance-shaped and 2 to 4 inches long. It grows in fields and forest edges.

The underground stems (rhizomes) of Solomon's seal were used in herbal medicine and as a food by Native Americans.

May-White

Lily-Of-The-Valley
Convallaria majalis

Family: ASPARAGACEAE

Strictly speaking, lily-of-the-valley is not a "wild" flower but is an ornamental that easily becomes naturalized; there is lots of it on Chebeague. The plant typically has a pair of broad, lance-shaped leaves, about 6 inches long, and a single flower stalk (6 to 10 inches long) bearing 10 to 12 tiny, bell-shaped, white flowers.

Lily-of-the-valley likes to grow in partial shade on our abundant sandy soils. It reproduces both with its berries (seeds) and by means of underground stems, so the plant can form dense stands.

All parts of lily-of-the-valley are toxic.

Common Dandelion
Taraxacum officinale

Family: ASTERACEAE

From 2 to 12 inches tall, this perennial is found in fields, lawns, and dis-turbed sites. Dandelions start flowering in May and flower abundantly in late spring, but some dandelions can be found in flower throughout the summer and into the fall. Each plant has a basal rosette of leaves, 3 to 12 inches long, and each lance-shaped leaf is divided into numerous pointed lobes. The flower heads are borne on a long stalk; each flower head consists of up to 100 individual flowers.

Dandelions are not native, but are of Eurasian origin. They were brought to the Americas for food (the flowers can be used to make wine and the leaves for salads), and are now found throughout North America.

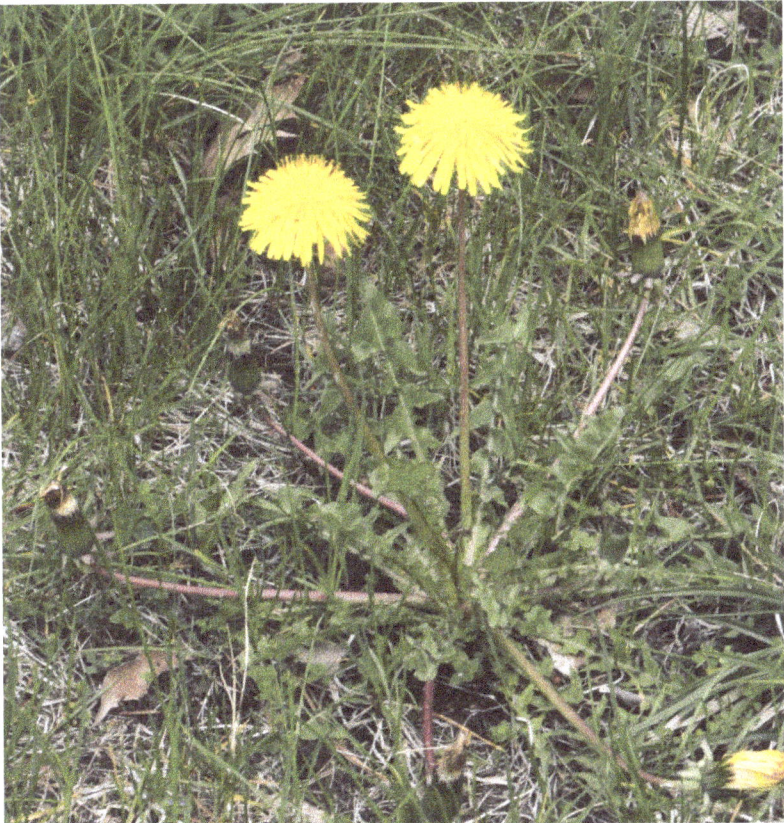

May-Yellow

Common Buttercup
Ranunculus acris

Family: RANUNCULACEAE

This familiar perennial is found in moist fields and roadside ditches. It is 1 to 3 feet tall, and the highly dissected leaves are easily identifiable. *R. acris* begins flowering in late May and continues to flower throughout the summer.

This plant is Eurasian in origin, but must have been introduced very early during European colonization as it was used by Native Americans as an herbal medicine. Buttercups are poisonous to humans but the poison is inactivated by heating or drying.

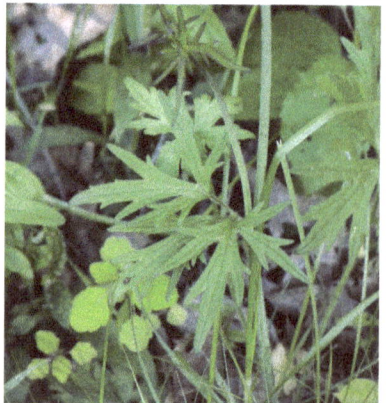

Dwarf Cinquefoil
Potentilla canadensis

Family: ROSACEAE

Dwarf cinquefoil is an annual, up to 6 inches tall, with yellow flowers about ½ inch in diameter, and leaves divided into 5 oval-shaped and toothed leaflets. It is similar in appearance to strawberry plants, but it produces a dry fruit not a fleshy one. This cinquefoil is found in dry sandy areas.

May-Yellow

Yellow Rocket, Winter Cress
Barbarea vulgaris

Family: BRASSICACEAE

Yellow rocket is 1 to 3 feet tall with many branches. The branches termi-nate in clusters of yellow flowers; each flower is no more than ½ inch long. The lower leaves are up to 4 inches long and deeply lobed; the upper leaves are smaller, clasp the stem, and end in pointed finger-like projec-tions.

Yellow rocket is a member of the mustard family (Brassicaceae). Mem-bers of this family are readily identified by their flowers and fruits. The flowers have four petals and six stamens; four long stamens and two shorter ones. The fruits (seed pods) are long and thin (called siliques).

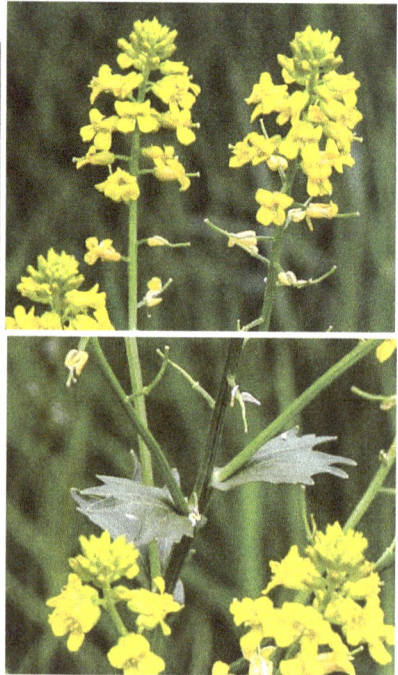

Pink Lady's Slipper
Cypripedium acaule

Family: ORCHIDACEAE

This is one of our woods' beauties and one protected by Maine law. It has a pair of ovate leaves, each 4 to 10 inches long, and when it flowers, a single stalk and flower are formed. The flowers are 3 to 4 inches long; the upper petals are lance-shaped and brown in color, the lower petals are pink or red and form a bulbous chamber. Flowering occurs only for a brief period in late spring.

May-Red/Pink

Dame's Rocket
Hesperis matronalis

Family: BRASSICACEAE

Dame's rocket grows in fields and ditches to a height of about 3 feet. The flowers, about ¾ inch across, have 4 pink or purple petals (sometimes white). The leaves are 4 to 6 inches long, lance-shaped, and have toothed margins. This plant resembles phlox, but phlox flowers have five petals, not four.

Red Clover
Trifolium pratense

Family: FABACEAE

Found in fields and lawns, red clover is usually 6 to 12 inches tall, with upright flowering stalks bearing clusters of small red flowers. Each leaf is divided into 3 lance-shaped leaflets that have distinct white chevrons. This plant starts to flower in May and continues to flower all summer. It is a great food source for butterflies and bees, and like all clovers, its roots fix nitrogen, which improves soil nutrition.

May-Red/Pink

Sheep Sorrel, Sheep Dock
Rumex acetosella

Family POLYGONACEAE

Sheep sorrel is an invasive garden pest but the young leaves are edible and can be added to salads. It is found in lawns, gardens, walkways, and driveways, and spreads by means of underground runners. When it flowers, it forms spikes (up to 1 foot tall) of tiny reddish or greenish flowers (green at first but maturing to red). The leaves are 2 to 4 inches long, and arrow-shaped with two lobes at the base.

Forget-Me-Not
Myosotis scorpioides

Family: BORAGINACEAE

Forget-me-not grows in moist fields, ditches, and roadsides. It is 1 to 2 feet tall, and forms clusters of flowers (½ inch across) with 5 blue petals and yellow centers. The leaves are about 2 inches long and oval. There are also some plants with pink flowers and some with white ones, which are probably genetic variants.

May-Blue/Purple

Bluet
Houstonia caerulea

Family: RUBIACEAE

Like forget-me-not, this plant grows in moist fields and roadsides. It is 6 inches tall with flowers ½ inch across that have blue petals and yellow centers. Unlike forget-me-not, each flower has 4 petals, not 5, and the leaves are less than an inch long. The petals are a very pale blue, almost white on some plants.

Grape Hyacinth
Muscari sp. (perhaps *neglectum*)

Family: ASPARAGACEAE

This is probably not a wildflower but an escaped ornamental. The plant is 6 to 8 inches tall with spikes of small, bell-shaped, blue flowers. The leaves are grass-like, long and thin. It grows from a bulb and will become naturalized in fields.

May-Blue/Purple

Blue Violets
Viola sagittata and *Viola sororia*

Family: VIOLACEAE

I have seen two different species of blue violets on the islands. Both grow in woodlands and shaded roadsides. They are 4 to 6 inches tall, with flowers about 1 inch across, lighter colored centers, and dark veins in the center of the lower petal.   The leaves of *Viola sagittata* (arrowhead violet) are oval to lance-shaped and up to 4 inches long. The leaves of *Viola sororia* (common blue violet) are heart-shaped and a bit shorter.

V. sagittata

V. sororia

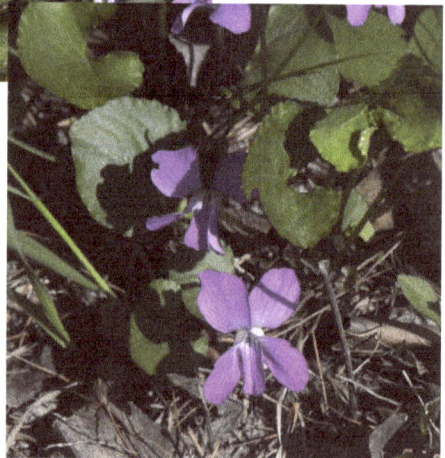

Jack-In-The-Pulpit
Arisaema triphyllum

Family: ARACEAE

Jack-in-the-pulpit grows in moist woods and shaded marshy areas. From 8 to 24 inches tall, the plant has 2 to 3 leaves, each of which is divided into 3 ovate leaflets. The 2- to 3-inch-long flower spike is a purple-brown rod (that's Jack, technically the spadix), and is surrounded by a cup-shaped leaf (the pulpit, technically the spathe) with purple-brown stripes and topped with a hood.

June-White

June brings the first taste of summer. Hawkweeds, ox-eye daisies, and yarrow burst out in our fields; our gardens come to life with peonies, irises, and gladiolas. Some of the flowers from May continue (dame's rocket, dandelion, wild lily-of-the-valley, and bunchberry), but they are fading.

Multiflora Rose or Rambler Rose
Rosa multiflora

Family: ROSACEAE

This shrub can be up to15 feet tall, climbing over other plants. Its white or pinkish flowers are 1 to 2 inches in diameter. Like one of our other wild roses, *Rosa rugosa*, multiflora rose is native to Asia, but was introduced to New England in the 19th century and is well established.

Mouse-Ear Chickweed
Cerastium fontanum

Family: CARYOPHYLLACEAE

We have two species of chickweed, mouse-ear chickweed and three-styled chickweed. Both are small plants. Mouse-ear chickweed is usually 5 to 10 inches tall, with small white flowers that have 5 petals, and each petal has two lobes. Mouse-ear chickweed has leaves that are lance-shaped and about twice as long as they are wide. The indentation that forms the lobes of each petal is about half the length of the petal.

Chickweed was introduced from Europe and grows in lawns, fields and gardens. It is edible and can be used in salads.

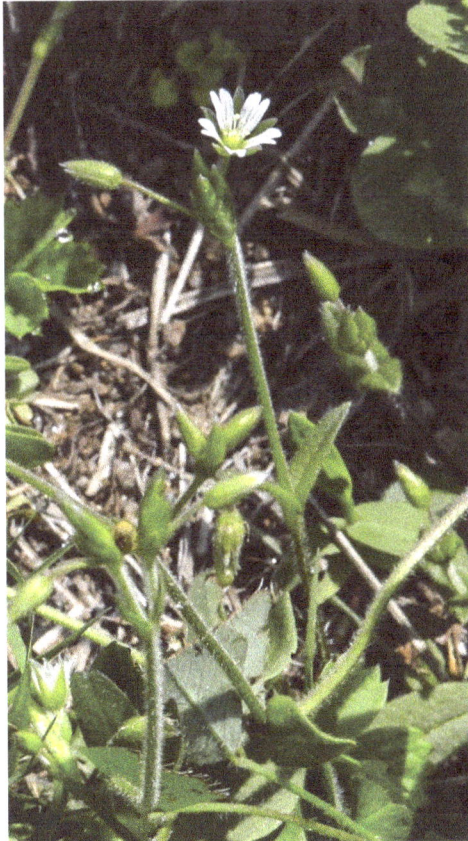

June-White

Three-Styled Chickweed or Doubtful Chickweed
Cerastium dubium

Family: CARYOPHYLLACEAE

This chickweed is longer than mouse-ear chickweed, has leaves that are more than twice as long as they are wide, and the indentation that forms the lobes of the petals almost divides each petal down its entire length. Also, if you examine the flowers with a strong hand lens you will find that the receptive surface of the female structure (the stigma and style) is divided into three lobes (hence the name three-styled chickweed). In contrast mouse-ear chickweed has the stigma and style divided into five lobes. The origin of the other name for this chickweed, doubtful chickweed, is a mystery to me.

White Clover
Trifolium repens

Family: FABACEAE

Familiar white clover grows in fields and lawns. It begins flowering in late spring and flowers throughout the summer. The plant grows 5 to10 inches high (unless mowed shorter!), with flower heads about 1 inch wide, and petals that are white or tinged pink. Each leaf is divided into three leaflets, which have faint white chevrons.

Originally from Eurasia, white clover is a very welcome invader as it harbors nitrogen-fixing bacteria in its roots, which improve soil nutrition.

June-White

Dropwort
Filipendula vulgaris

Family: ROSACEAE

This plant has a cluster of small white flowers at the top of a bare stalk that is 2 to 3 feet tall. At the base are fern-like leaves. Dropwort is found in dry fields. The common name apparently refers to rounded projections from the roots.

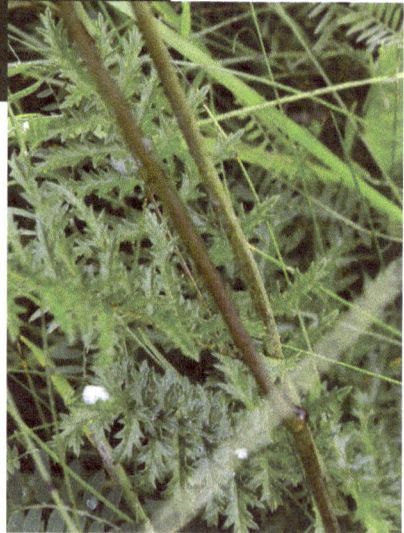

Cow Parsnip
Heracleum maximum

Family: APIACEAE

Cow parsnip is a large plant in the carrot family, growing 4 to 6 feet tall. It is found in fields. The flower heads are 8 to 10 inches across. The leaves are a foot and a half long, and are divided into three toothed leaflets.

The young flower stalks are said to be edible, but the juice from older leaves and stems can cause a rash.

June-White

Ox-Eye Daisy
Leucanthemum vulgare (formerly *Chrysanthemum leucanthemum*)

Family: ASTERACEAE

This perennial is up to 3 feet tall, with flower heads about 2 inches in diameter. Each flower stalk bears a single flower head, which has about 30 white petals (ray flowers) and a yellow center (disc flowers). The leaves on the flower stalk are about 2 inches long, and are narrow and lance-shaped.

Ox-eye daisy grows in fields and roadside ditches and, along with yarrow, is one of the signature wildflowers of June.

Daisy Fleabane
Erigeron strigosus

Family: ASTERACEAE

Up to 3 feet tall with flowers about ½ inch across, daisy fleabane is an annual plant that grows in fields and roadside ditches. It has lance-shaped leaves that are 2 to 4 inches long. Its flower heads are smaller than those of ox-eye daisy, and the flower stalks are branched and may have 15 or more flower heads.

June-White

Yarrow
Achillea millefolium

Family: ASTERACEAE

To me, yarrow is a signature wildflower for late spring and early summer. It is a perennial growing up to 3 feet tall, with clusters of tiny white flowers, and highly dissected fern-like leaves. Occasionally you will find plants with pink flowers rather than white.

Yarrow was used in herbal medicine as an astringent and a tonic. It has also been domesticated for gardening; many horticultural varieties are available.

Whorled Bedstraw
Galium mollugo

Family: RUBIACEAE

This perennial grows in fields and roadside areas. It often grows in great masses, with each plant 3 or more feet long and sprawling over the grass and weeds in the field. The tiny white flowers, about ¼ inch across, have four petals. The lance-shaped leaves are formed in whorls at each node, with 5 to 8 leaves in each whorl. Leaves at the younger nodes may be ½ inch long or less; at older nodes the leaves may be over 2 inches long. A second species may be present (northern bedstraw, *Galium boreale*), which looks very similar but has only 4 leaves in the whorls at each node.

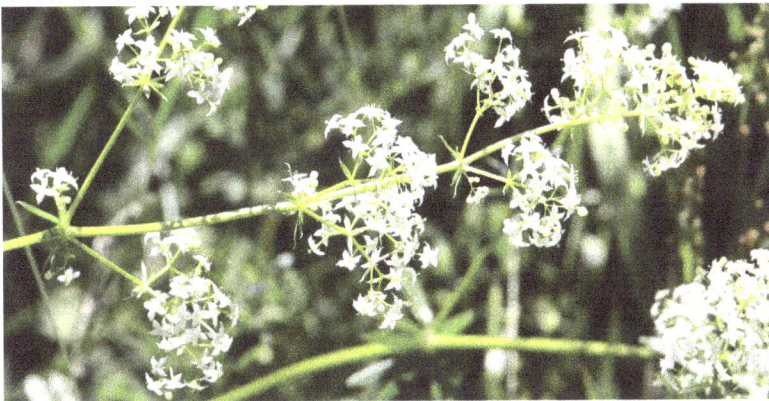

39

June-Yellow

Yellow Rattle
Rhinanthus minor

Family: OROBANCHACEAE

An annual plant about one foot tall, it is found in fields. The flowers are about ½ inch long, with yellow petals emerging from an inflated base. Yellow rattle is easy to overlook but quite attractive when you look closely.

This plant is partially parasitic and gets some of its nutrition from the roots of neighboring plants. All members of the family Orobanchaceae are partially or fully parasitic.

Mouse-Ear Hawkweed
Hieracium pilosella

Family: ASTERACEAE

Mouse-ear hawkweed is from 5 to 15 inches tall, with flowers about 1 inch in diameter, and a basal cluster of ovate and hairy leaves. Each plant has a single unbranched flower stalk. This plant grows in lawns and fields, particularly in drier sites. Mouse-ear hawkweed superficially resembles dandelion but the leaves are entire, not dissected into numerous sharp-toothed lobes, and its seeds are not wind dispersed in a puff.

Mouse-ear hawkweed is a major component of dry lawns. It flowers intensely in June, but some flowers will be found throughout the summer. In June it can cover our lawns with a carpet of yellow flowers.

June-Yellow

Yellow Hawkweed, Yellow King-Devil
Hieracium caespitosum

Family: ASTERACEAE

This hawkweed is up to 3 feet tall and each plant produces several branched flower stalks. It has a basal cluster of lance-shaped leaves 3 to 7 inches long. Yellow hawkweed is found in fields and along the roads; unlike mouse-ear hawkweed, yellow hawkweed does not tolerate mowing well and won't grow in lawns. We have a third species of hawkweed which has orange flowers -- orange hawkweed -- look for it with the orange flowers of June.

Silver Cinquefoil
Potentilla argentea

Family: ROSACEAE

Silver cinquefoil grows in dry lawns and driveways; sandy dry sites. It is 3 to 12 inches tall, with the leaves divided into 5 leaflets like a hand. The leaflets are about 1 inch long and the margins are toothed. The upper surfaces of the leaves are bright green, but their undersides are distinctly white or silvery due to the presence of fine white hairs. The flowers are about ½ inch across and have 5 yellow petals.

June-Yellow

Bird's-Foot Trefoil
Lotus corniculatus

Family: FABACEAE

Found on roadsides and in ditches, bird's-foot trefoil grows 6 to 8 inches tall. The flowers are formed in clusters of 5 or more individual flowers that are less than 1 inch long. Each leaf is divided into 5 leaflets; the upper 3 resemble clover, but then there are two more small leaflets at the base of the petiole. This plant is often found growing in large clusters; one is on the road down to the Hook on Chebeague. When young, the flowers are yellow; as they age, they turn orange.

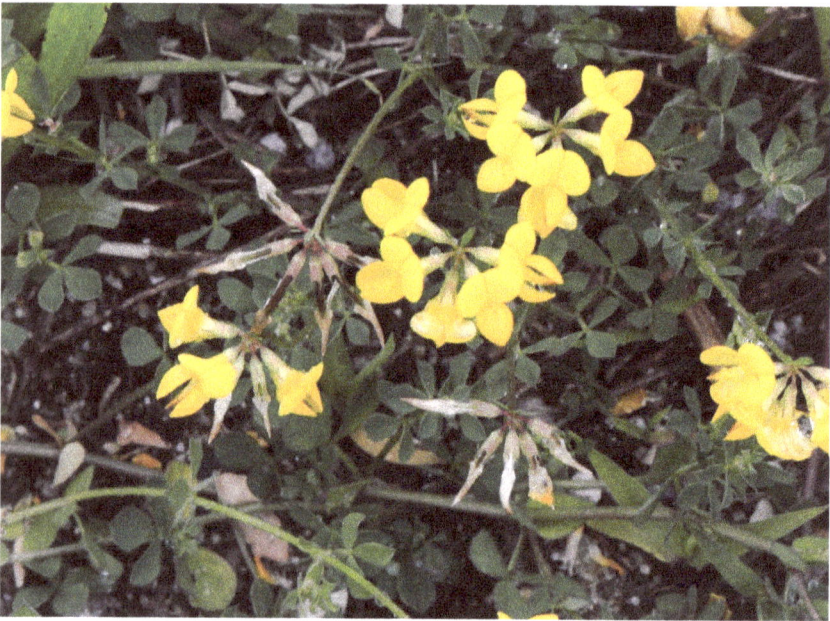

Orange Hawkweed, Orange King-Devil
Hieracium aurantiacum

Family: ASTERACEAE

Found in fields and along the roads, orange hawkweed is up to 15 inches tall. The flower stalks usually have several flower heads, with startling orange petals. Each flower head is ½ to ¾ of an inch in diameter. There is a basal cluster of lance-shaped leaves, each 3 to 6 inches long.

My father called this plant Indian paintbrush, but that name is usually used for another plant (a species of *Castilleja*), which occurs in the Western U.S. Orange hawkweed is a better name for *H. aurantiacum*.

June-Red/Pink

Ragged-Robin
Lychnis flos-cuculi

Family: CARYOPHYLLACEAE

Ragged-robin grows up to 3 feet tall, and forms loose clusters of flowers, with highly dissected pink petals. The flowers are 1 to 1½ inches in diameter. This plant grows in fields and thickets.

Crown Vetch
Securigera varia

Family: FABACEAE

Crown vetch grows in dense colonies in fields and roadsides. It is up to 2 feet tall, with flower clusters 1½ inches in diameter; the individual flowers are less than ½ inch long and have some pink and some white petals. The leaves are several inches long and are divided into many leaflets. Crown vetch is weedy, and can be a nuisance plant, but its flowers are quite attractive. Flowering begins in June and continues throughout the summer.

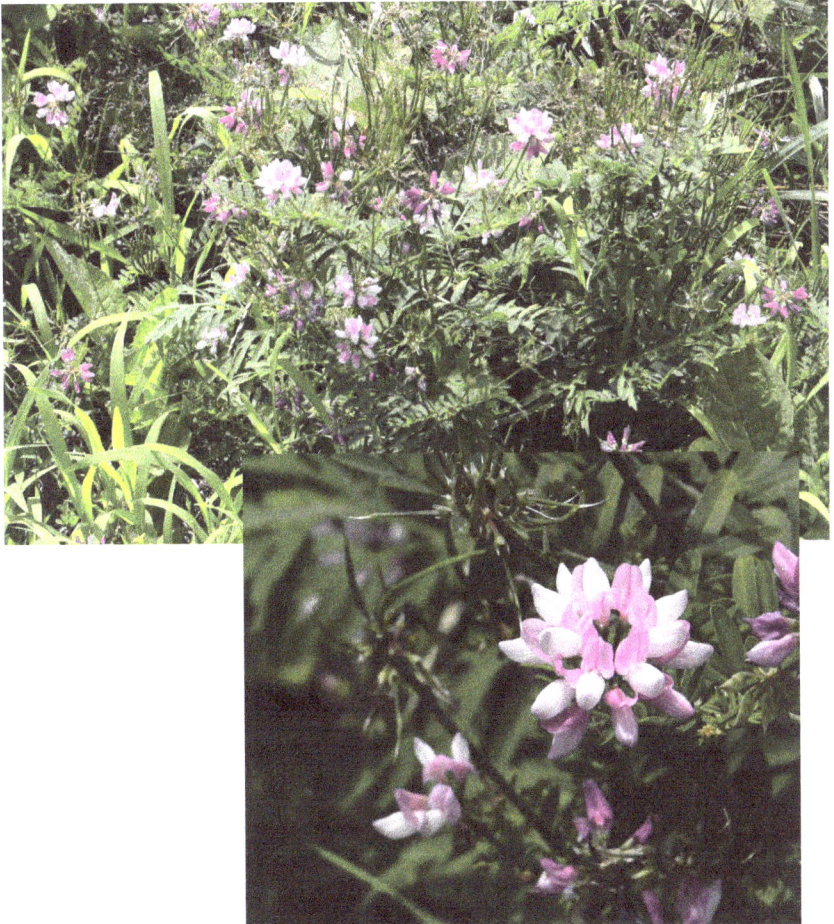

47

June-Red/Pink

Beach Pea
Lathyrus maritimus

Family: FABACEAE

Beach pea is found in sandy areas at the edge of beaches. It is up to 2 feet tall, and forms clusters of purple flowers. The leaves are divided into many individual leaflets, each of which is 1 to 2 inches long.

The pods of beach pea can be eaten, but consumption of large quantities can cause lathyrism (paralysis of the lower limbs).

Rabbit-Foot Clover
Trifolium arvense

Family: FABACEAE

Rabbit-foot clover is 5 to 15 inches tall, with pinkish flower clusters, which are 1 to 1½ inches long and ½ inch wide. The leaves are divided into three leaflets that are ½ to 1 inch long.

Rabbit-foot clover is typically found along roadsides and other areas that are lacking other plants. Flowering begins in June and continues through-out the summer.

June-Red/Pink

Foxglove
Digitalis purpurea

Family: PLANTAGINACEAE

Growing to a height of 3 feet, this plant is a popular ornamental that can escape cultivation. Its tubular flowers are 1 to 2 inches long, and the leaves are lance-shaped and 4 to 8 inches long.

Foxglove is native to Europe, and extracts from foxglove have been used for centuries to treat congestive heart failure.

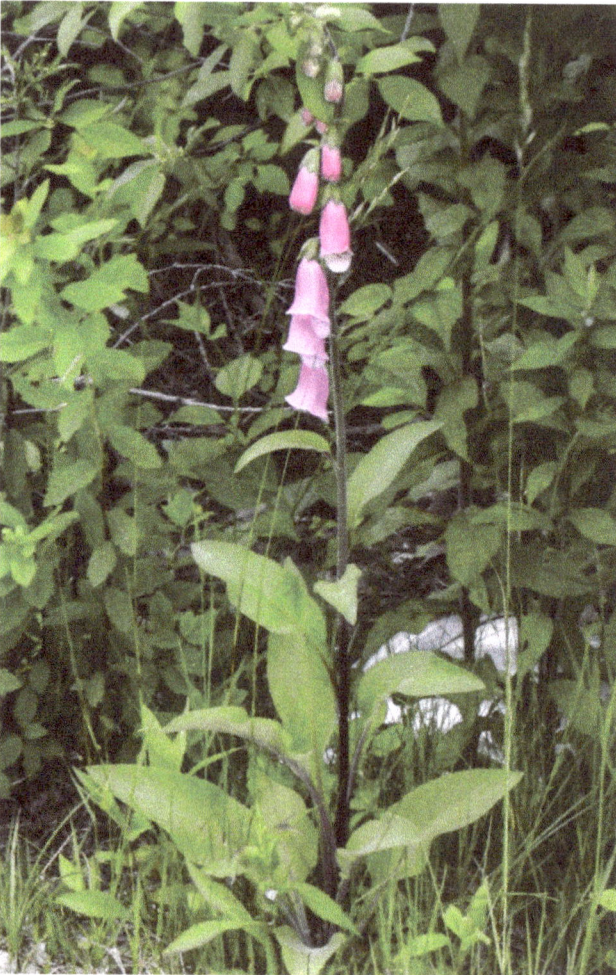

Morning Glory, Hedge Bindweed
Calystegia sepium

Family: CONVOLVULACEAE

This is a perennial vine found at the edges of salt marshes and beaches. The heart-shaped leaves are 3 to 4 inches long, and the pink and white flowers are 2 to 3 inches across. This photo was taken on the road to the Hook on Chebeague.

June-Red/Pink

Twinflower
Linnaea borealis

Family: CAPRIFOLIACEAE

Twinflower is found in our spruce woods. Each plant has a rosette of ovate leaves, up to 1 inch long, and produces a flowering stalk that ends in a pair of delicate, ½-inch-long, pink flowers. It grows in carpet-like masses. Flowering lasts for less than two weeks in June, so you have to keep an eye out for it. But, it's a perennial, so once you have found it, you can enjoy it every year.

Twinflower is found worldwide in the northern boreal forests. Wikipedia says it was Linnaeus' favorite flower -- it is certainly mine, too. The photo was taken on the Roy Hill Road near the Second Wind Farm on Chebeague.

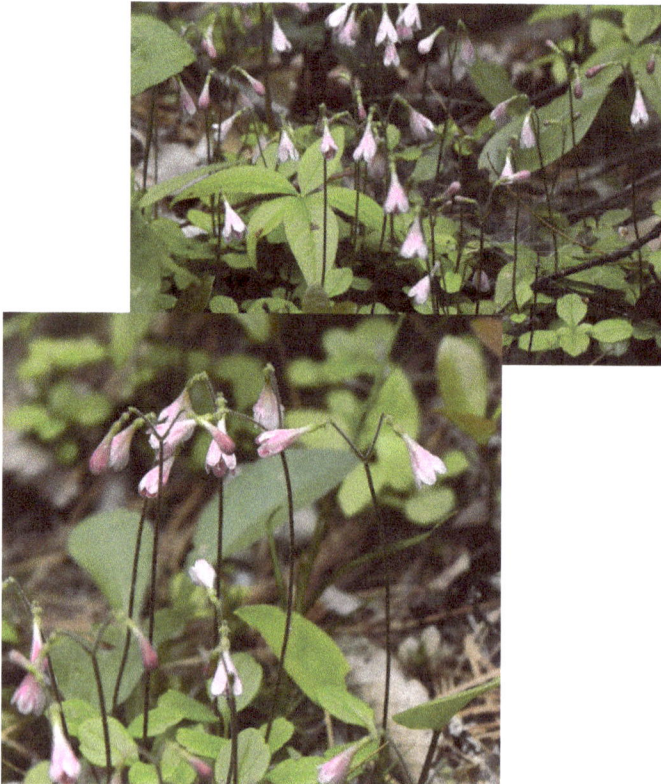

Blue Vetch, Cow Vetch
Vicia cracca

Family: FABACEAE

This plant is a nasty weed, but its flowers are pretty. Blue vetch grows in fields, gardens, and roadsides. It can be up to 5 feet long, and grows twining over other plants. The flower clusters contain as many as 30, half-inch-long, blue flowers. The leaves have 15 to 30 one-inch-long leaflets.

Like most members of the pea family, blue vetch is a nitrogen-fixing plant, so it has its positive side. Flowering begins in June and continues into the fall.

June-Blue/Purple

Blue Flag Iris, Northern Blue Iris
Iris versicolor

Family: IRIDACEAE

This popular ornamental is also a native wildflower. Probably most of the irises growing on the islands outside of gardens are escaped ornamentals, but who knows? The plant grows to be 3 feet tall with flowers 3 to 4 inches across.

Blue-Eyed Grass
Sisyrinchium angustifolium

Family: IRIDACEAE

This sweet plant grows in fields and roadsides to a height of 8 to 12 inches. The flowers are about ½ inch across, and form on the tips of long flat stems. The leaves are long, thin and flattened, resembling grass, although the plant is not related to grasses.

June-Blue/Purple

Lupine, Garden Lupine
Lupinus polyphyllus

Family: FABACEAE

This showy favorite grows wild throughout Maine, but it was introduced from the western U.S. It grows well in gardens and easily escapes. Lupine is 3 to 4 feet tall, with flowering spikes 12 to 16 inches long. The individual flowers are up to 1 inch long. Each leaf is divided into a palm-like structure with 12 or more long, lance-shaped, leaflets.

Bittersweet, Asian Bittersweet
Celastrus orbiculatus

Family: CELASTRACEAE

Bittersweet is the worst exotic invasive plant on the islands. This fast-growing vine will grow over shrubs and trees and take over fields. Bittersweet has tiny flowers with green petals, and forms red berries in the fall. The birds love the berries and spread bittersweet seeds throughout the environment.

Controlling bittersweet is very difficult. Frequent mowing will keep it out of fields, because the roots will eventually die. But at forest edges and among shrubs, simply cutting off the stems is not effective; bittersweet vines will grow back. Pulling up the vines helps, but it is difficult to pull up all the roots. If you are diligent and persistent in cutting and pulling, over a period of years, it can eventually be controlled. Should you decide to use chemical control, the best herbicide to use is Roundup. The safest, and most effective, way to use Roundup on bittersweet is to cut the vines near the ground and paint the cut stems with Roundup concentrate. The chemical is absorbed down into the roots and kills them. When using Roundup, care must be taken to apply it only to the target plant and to keep it out of waterways.

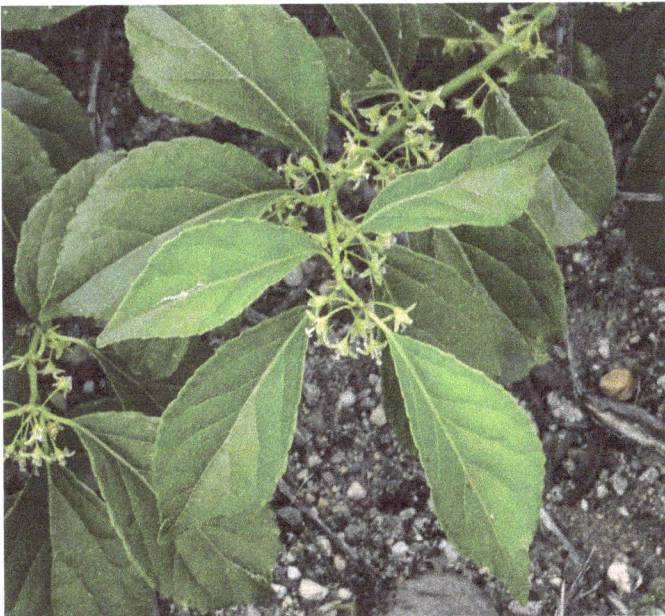

July/August-White

July and August are high summer and our fields become crowded with black-eyed Susans, Queen Anne's lace, meadowsweet, goldenrod, thistles, and St. Johnswort. Some new things flower in the woods too. Toward the end of August, the transition to the fall flowers begins, with goldenrods and asters taking over.

The clovers, blue vetch, yarrow, hawkweeds, cinquefoils, and dandelion continue to be seen but are flowering less intensely. Ox-eye daisies are fading.

White Campion
Silene latifolia

Family: CARYOPHYLLACEAE

Growing up to 3 feet, white campion has flowers ¾ inch wide, with white petals, and distinctive inflated green bases. The leaves are several inches long, lance-shaped, and lack petioles. White campion is found in fields.

Meadowsweet
Spiraea alba

Family: ROSACEAE

Meadowsweet is a shrub, 2 to 5 feet tall, with spikes of tiny flowers less than ¼ inch wide. The petals are white; the flower centers are pinkish at first and fade to brown. Meadowsweet grows in fields and marshy sites.

July/August-White

Queen Anne's Lace, Wild Carrot
Daucus carota

Family: APIACEAE

Wild carrot is 1 to 3 feet tall and terminates in a 2- to 4-inch-wide, flat-topped cluster of tiny, 1/8-inch-diameter, white flowers. This flower arrangement is called an umbel and is characteristic of members of the carrot family. The leaves are highly dissected and may be as much as 10 inches long.

Wild carrot is of Eurasian origin and is the plant from which domesticated carrots arose. Most of the flower clusters have a single central flower with purple petals, probably to attract pollinators.

Purple Flower

July/August-White

American Black Elderberry
Sambucus canadensis

Family: ADOAXACEAE

Elderberry is a deciduous shrub up to 15 feet tall that forms clusters of small white flowers. Each leaf has 7 to 9 leaflets, which are each 3 to 4 inches long. The berries that form in late summer are black.

The cooked ripe berries are edible, but unripe berries and other parts of the plant are toxic. Juice from the berries has long been used to treat colds and flu, and I've been told that my great grandmother, Susan Bates, made elderberry wine. This photo was taken in front of the house where Susan lived on Chebeague's South Road; could the bush have been there all these years?

July/August-White

English Plantain, Narrowleaf Plantain
Plantago lanceolata

Family: PLANTAGINACEAE

This lawn and field weed is an import from Europe. The narrow lance-shaped leaves are 4 to 12 inches long with prominent ribs running their length. The tiny white flowers are formed on a spike at the end of a stalk that can be 1½ feet tall.

Along with broad-leaf plantain, the young leaves are edible; the leaves have also been used in herbal medicine teas.

Shineleaf Pyrola, Elliptic-Leaved Pyrola
Pyrola elliptica

Family: ERICACEAE

This woodland plant has a basal rosette of leaves and a flowering stalk 10 to 12 inches tall. It grows beneath pines and, unlike most of our woodland wildflowers, which flower in the spring, shineleaf pyrola flowers in mid to late July.

Shineleaf pyrola is in the same plant family as blueberries, heather, rhododendrons, and azaleas. Plants in this family have urn-shaped flowers, with 5 sepals, 5 petals, and 10 stamens. One unusual feature of plants in this family is that their anthers (pollen sacs) have a pore at the tip (visible with a hand lens).

July/August-White

Checkerberry, wintergreen
Gaultheria procumbens

Family: ERICACEAE

Checkerberry is rarely more than 2 or 3 inches tall and grows at the edge of the woods. The flowers are less than ½ inch long, with white petals, and resemble the flowers of blueberries, which are in the same family. Checkerberry's leaves are oval-shaped and 1 to 2 inches long.

My father introduced me to this plant, as a young boy, by having me chew the leaves; they have a refreshing but astringent taste.

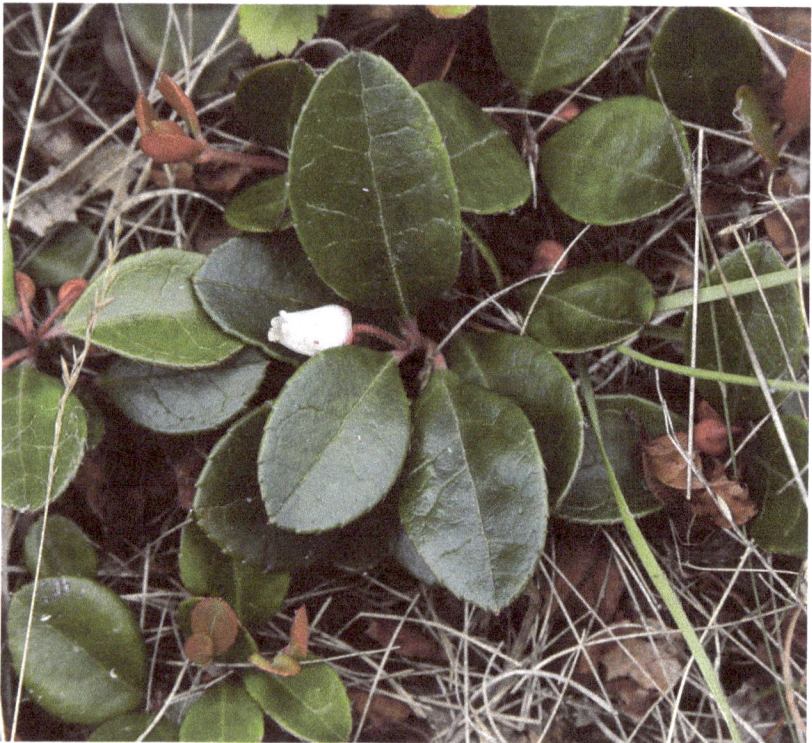

Indian Pipe
Monotropa uniflora

Family: ERICACEAE

Like shineleaf pyrola, this plant is also in the blueberry family, but it is totally parasitic/saprophytic. The only part of the plant to be seen above ground is the flowering stalk, which is 8 to 12 inches tall, and each stalk ends with a single flower -- hence the scientific name uniflora. The flowering stalks have small scaly leaves, but the plants contain no chlorophyll and are completely unable to photosynthesize.

Indian pipe grows in association with pines, spruces, and beech trees, and it was once believed that it parasitized the roots of those trees, drawing its nutrition from them directly. Now it has been found that the relationship is more complex and involves a fungus as an intermediary. The roots of forest trees are associated with fungi, called mycorrhizal fungi, whose filaments penetrate the tree roots. The fungi obtain their nutrition from the tree roots and in return provide the trees with better access to mineral elements, particularly phosphorus. These mycorrhizal fungi interconnect the trees in the forest making the forest, in a sense, one continuous organism. Indian pipe piggybacks off this relationship. The mycorrhizal fungi penetrate the roots of Indian pipe plants, which then get their nutrition from the forest trees through the fungi as intermediaries.

July/August-White

Pinesap
Monotropa hypopitys

Family: ERICACEAE

Pinesap grows in pine/spruce forests and, like Indian pipe, it is parasitic and lacks chlorophyll. The plant is 5-10 inches tall, with scale-like leaves and a cluster of flowers at the tip of each stalk. See the entry for Indian pipe for information about the nutrition of these plants.

Dodder
Cuscuta gronovii

Family: Convolvulaceae

Dodder is a true parasite. Its thread-like orange stems can be 6 feet long. The stems wrap around host plants, and then send out minute side branches that penetrate the host plant and draw out nutrients. The plant is not leafless, but has tiny scale-like leaves. But it lacks chlorophyll, is unable to photosynthesize, and obtains all its nutrition from its host. Dodder forms clusters of tiny (1/8 inch-across) flowers, each with 5 white petals.

Dodder can grow on a wide range of host plants; in some areas it can be a serious agricultural pest.

July/August-White

Common Milkweed
Asclepias syriaca

Family: APOCYNACEAE

Milkweed is 2 to 4 feet tall and prefers sunny sites and sandy soils. The flowers are formed in clusters of small (½-inch-long) individual flowers with pinkish white petals.

Milkweed is fed on by many insects, but it is the sole food source of monarch butterfly caterpillars. Maintaining a good supply of this plant is key to the survival of monarchs. The relationship between the monarchs and milkweed is an interesting example of species interactions. Milkweeds, particularly the older plants, produce a white latex filled with bitter compounds. The monarch caterpillars concentrate these bitter compounds in their bodies making themselves, and monarch butterflies, unpalatable to birds. The bright colors of the monarch caterpillars and butterflies are a warning notice to birds that they are not good to eat.

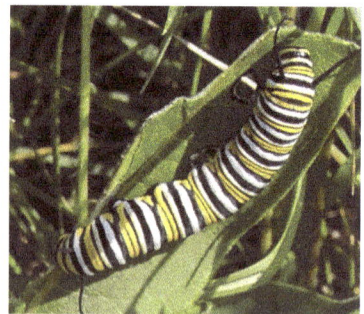

Three-Leaved Rattlesnake-Root
Nabalus trifoliolatus

Family: ASTERACEAE

Three-leaved rattlesnake-root is found in woodland edges and roadsides, and grows 3 to 4 feet tall. The flower stalk is branched and terminates in clusters of drooping flowers with white petals. The leaves are about 4 inches long and each leaf is divided into three leaflets. The central leaflet has three lobes; the two lower leaflets each have two lobes.

July/August-White

Corn Chamomile, Scentless Chamomile
Anthemis arvensis

Family: ASTERACEAE

This plant is of European origin and those on Chebeague may be escaped ornamentals. It grows in fields; the one in this photo was on the bank above the shore below Cordes Road on Chebeague. The plant is 2 to 3 feet tall, with daisy-like, white flowers (about 1 inch across) with yellow centers. The leaves are distinctive; they are finely divided into thin finger-like filaments, reminiscent of dill.

Boneset
Eupatorium perfoliatum

Family: ASTERACEAE

Boneset is found in wet roadside ditches and marshy areas. It grows 3 to 5 feet tall and has clusters of small white flowers at the top of the stalks. The leaves are opposite, lance-shaped and up to 6 inches long.

Boneset was used by Native Americans and European colonists to treat fevers and promote the healing of broken bones.

July/August-White

Arrow-Leaved Tearthumb
Persicaria sagittata

Family: POLYGONACEAE

Arrow-leaved tearthumb grows in marshy, wet places; you will frequently see it in roadside ditches. The plant grows along the ground and may be several feet long, but is rarely over 1 foot tall. The stems appear jointed (a feature of members of the family Polygonaceae) and at each node there is an arrow-shaped leaf, 3 to 4 inches long, that clasps the stem. The stems terminate in a cluster of small white flowers, each about 1/8 inch long.

The stems and the backs of the leaves have short sharp spines, hence the plant's name, tearthumb. Try handling it and you will see!

Creeping Buttercup
Ranunculus repens

Family: RANUNCULACEAE

Creeping buttercup is found in moist, wet habitats -- fields and ditches. The plant is generally about 1 foot tall, with bright yellow flowers 1 inch across. The leaves are palm-shaped and are divided into three toothed-leaflets each about 2 inches long. It is the shape of the leaves that distinguishes it from the common buttercup. Creeping buttercup, like common buttercup, is native to Europe.

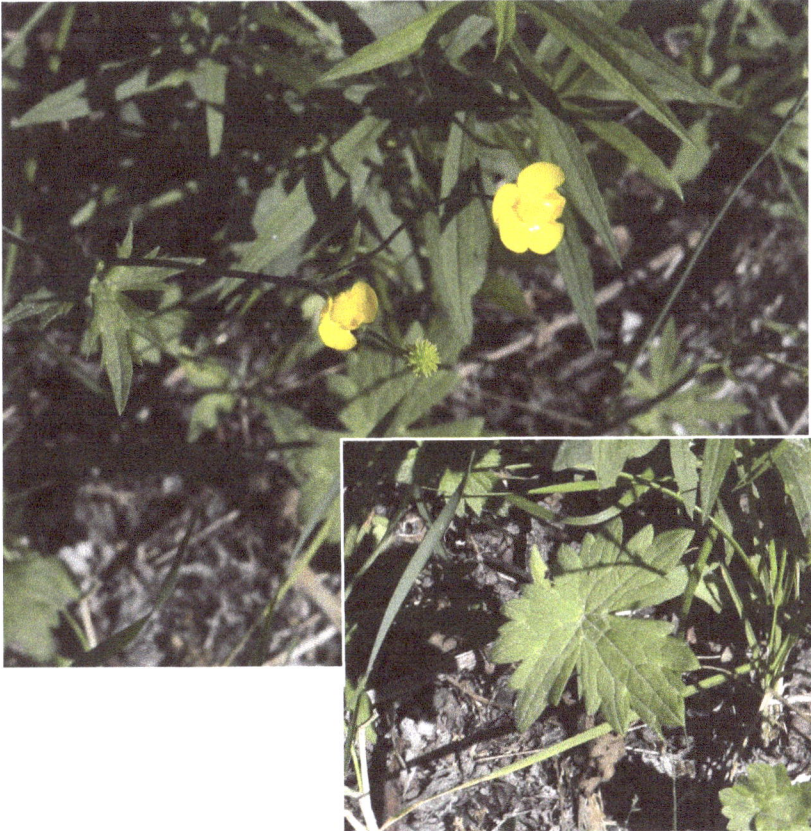

July/August-Yellow

Black Mustard
Brassica nigra

Family: BRASSICACEAE

Black mustard is a many-branched scraggly plant 2 to 3 feet tall, with loose clusters of yellow flowers. Each flower has four petals (as do all species in the mustard family). The flowers are ½ to ¾ inch across. The lower leaves are 3 to 4 inches long, attached to the stem with a petiole (a stalk), and have two or more lobes at the base. Black mustard is said to grow in disturbed sites; on Chebeague it is often found near the beaches.

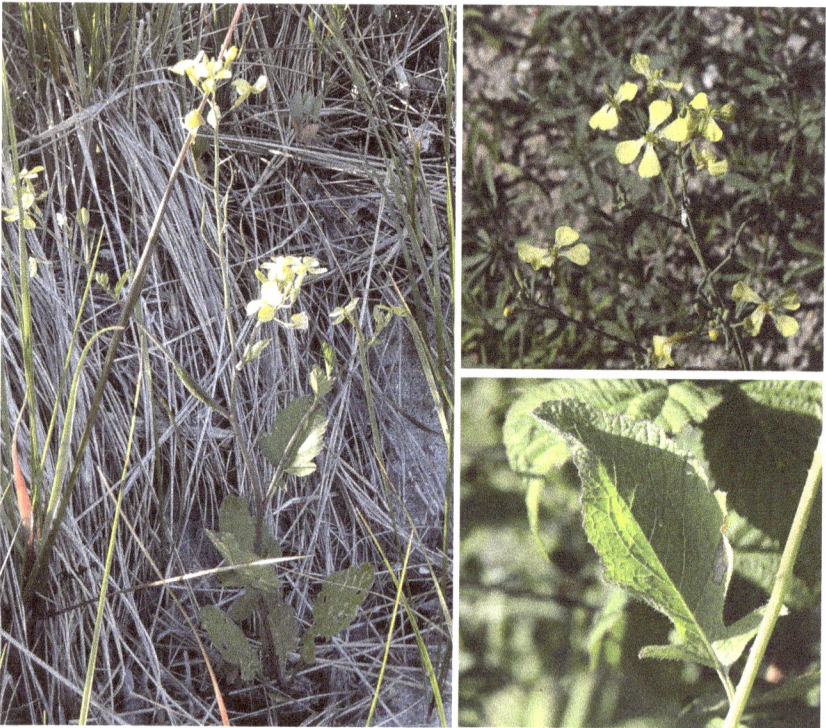

Common Wood Sorrel
Oxalis stricta

Family: OXALIDACEAE

Found in fields, lawns and garden beds, wood sorrel is a persistent weed, but does have pretty yellow flowers. The plants are usually about 6 inches tall, and the flowers are about ½ inch across. The leaves, ½ to 1 inch across, are divided into three heart-shaped leaflets. Wood sorrel can be confused with clover because of its three leaflets. However, the flowers are very different than those of clovers, and the leaflets on wood sorrel are strongly notched, whereas those on clover are not.

Wood sorrel, which is sometimes called sourgrass, is edible and has a sour but pleasant taste. However, it should not be eaten in large amounts because the compound that gives its sour taste, oxalic acid, inhibits calcium absorption.

Hop Clover, Low Hop Clover
Trifolium campestre

Family: FABACEAE

This plant likes disturbed sites, so it is frequently found in roadside ditches. It grows to about 1 foot tall and its tiny, yellow, pea-shaped flowers, are clustered in heads of 15 to 20 individual flowers. Each leaf is divided into three, ½-inch-long, ovate leaflets.

Rough-Fruited Cinquefoil
Potentilla recta

Family: ROSACEAE

This cinquefoil has its leaves divided into 5 to 7 lance-shaped leaflets that are toothed all along their margins; individual leaflets may be up to 3 inches long. The plants are 1 to 2 feet tall. The flowers are about 1 inch across with pale yellow petals. This is the largest of our cinquefoils and, like our other cinquefoils, is found in open fields.

Cow-Wheat
Melampyrum lineare

Family: OROBANCHACEAE

Cow-wheat is found in the shaded edges of the woods. It is about 1 foot tall and has opposite leaves that are lance-shaped and up to 2 inches long. Its flowers are tubular, about 1 inch long, and have yellow lips. Cow-wheat is a semiparasite, obtaining some of its nutrition from the roots of other plants, a characteristic of all members of the Orobanchaceae.

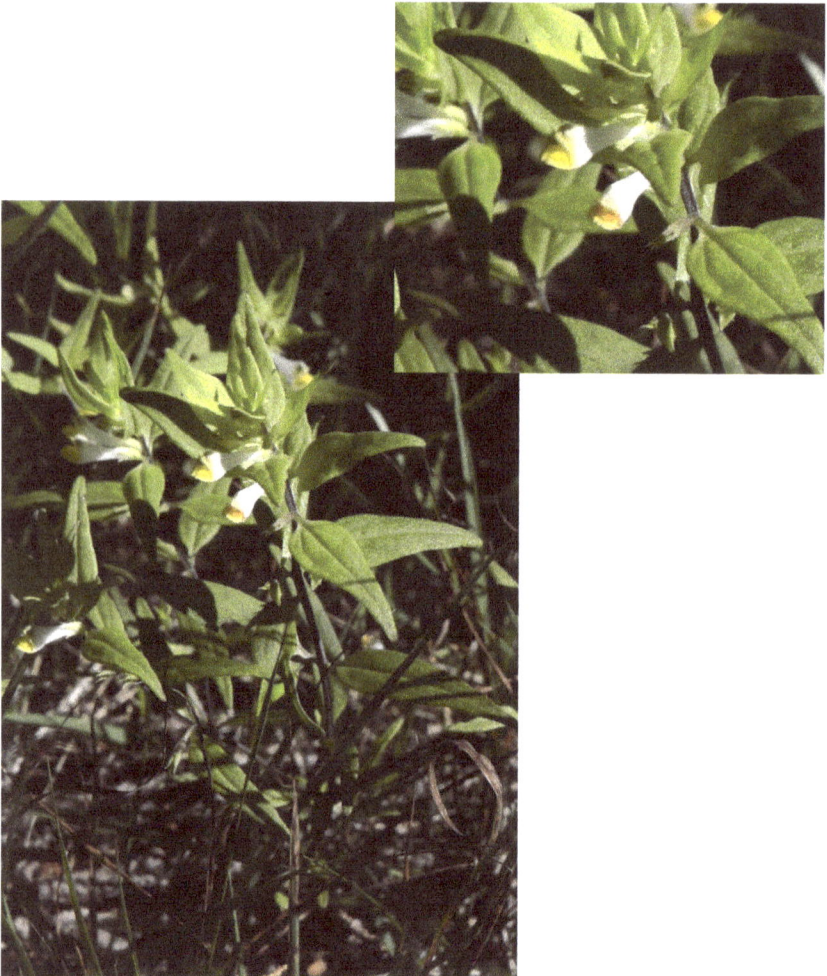

Common Mullein
Verbascum thapsus

Family: SCHROPHULARIACEAE

Common mullein is found in fields and roadside ditches. The plant can be 5 to 6 feet tall. It has lance-shaped leaves that may be as much as 1 foot long and covered with fine velvety hairs. The flowers form on a long spike and are about 1 inch long. Each individual flower opens only for a single day. Although not very handsome, this plant is certainly striking due to its size and unusual appearance.

Common mullein is a Eurasian plant that is now found throughout the world. It has a long history of use in herbal medicine for treatment of lung and throat disorders and was introduced into North America in the early 1700s for medicinal use.

July/August-Yellow

Northern Evening Primrose
Oenothera parviflora

Family: ONAGRACEAE

Northern evening primrose can be up to 5 feet tall. It has alternate leaves, several inches long, that are lance-shaped with finely toothed margins and short or missing petioles. The flowers are 1 to 2 inches long.

Northern evening primrose is found in dry sites in fields, roadside ditches, and near buildings. This photo was taken by our barn door.

Yellow Loosestrife, Swamp Yellow Loosestrife
Lysimachia terrestris

Family: MYRSINACEAE

One of two loosestrifes I have seen on the islands, yellow loosestrife grows in wet fields and roadside ditches. The plant is generally 2 feet tall, with the last foot a spike of yellow flowers with red centers. The flowers are about 1 inch across, and the lance-shaped leaves are 2 to 4 inches long.

Whorled Loosestrife
Lysimachia quadrifolia

Family: MYRSINACEAE

Whorled loosestrife grows in drier and shadier sites than yellow loose-strife. Look for it in woodland edges and wooded roadsides. It is generally about 2 feet tall and has flowers less than 1 inch across. Unlike yellow loosestrife, which has alternate leaves, whorled loosestrife forms a whorl of leaves at each node. The upper nodes of the plant also form a whorl of yellow flowers with attractive red centers. Despite its scientific name (quadrifolia), many of the plants I have seen have three or five leaves per whorl rather than four.

St. John's-Wort, Common St. John's-Wort
Hypericum perforatum

Family: HYPERICACEAE

St. John's-wort grows 2 to 3 feet tall and is found in fields and roadsides. The plant is highly branched, and each flowering shoot terminates in a single, 1 inch-wide, flower with five bright yellow petals and a large number of stamens. The leaves are also about 1 inch long and are opposite and narrowly ovate.

St. John's-wort has long been used in herbal medicine and is currently used as a treatment for depression. Clinical studies of its effectiveness have been inconsistent. Studies conducted by ConsumerLab.com found commercially available preparations of St. John's-wort varied greatly in the amount of the active ingredient (hyperforin) they contained, which may account for the inconsistency of the clinical study results. People taking St John's-wort should also be aware that it reduces the effectiveness of a range of prescription drugs including commonly prescribed statins and beta-blockers. (https://nccih.nih.gov/health/stjohnswort/ataglance.htm)

Black-Eyed Susan
Rudbeckia hirta

Family: ASTERACEAE

For me, this plant, along with Queen Anne's lace and yarrow, is an icon of summer on the islands. Growing in fields and roadsides, black-eyed Susan is 2 to 3 feet tall, and the flower head is about 3 inches across. Like all members of its family (Asteraceae, the sunflower family), the "flower" of black-eyed Susan is actually a complicated collection of many individual flowers. The dark central disk is a densely packed collection of tiny flowers that have greatly reduced petals; these are called disc flowers and are almost invisible to the naked eye. The outer flowers each have a single greatly enlarged petal (these flowers are called ray flowers). Black-eyed Susan is a popular ornamental.

Tansy, Common Tansy
Tanacetum vulgare

Family: ASTERACEAE

Tansy grows 4 to 5 feet tall; its habitat is dry fields and roadsides. The flower heads are compact, about ½ inch across and composed of many disc flowers with tiny yellow petals. Tansy has no ray flowers. The leaves are 4 to 6 inches long and are deeply divided into many leaflets.

Tansy is native to Eurasia and was introduced into North America by early colonists for use as an herbal medicine. It is no longer considered an effective herbal medicine and is toxic at high concentrations.

There is a lot of tansy along the roadside at the West End of Chebeague, across the road from the Sanford's skating pond. Perhaps it is an escaped ornamental there.

July/August-Yellow

Early Goldenrod
Solidago juncea

Family: ASTERACEAE

As its name suggests, this is the first of the goldenrods to flower. It grows 1 to 3 feet tall, with curving flower clusters at the ends of the stalks. The individual flowers are quite small, 1/8 inch across. The leaves are oval to lance-shaped, 1 to 6 inches long, and the surfaces of the leaves are smooth, with no obvious leaf veins except the midrib. Early goldenrod is found in fields and roadsides.

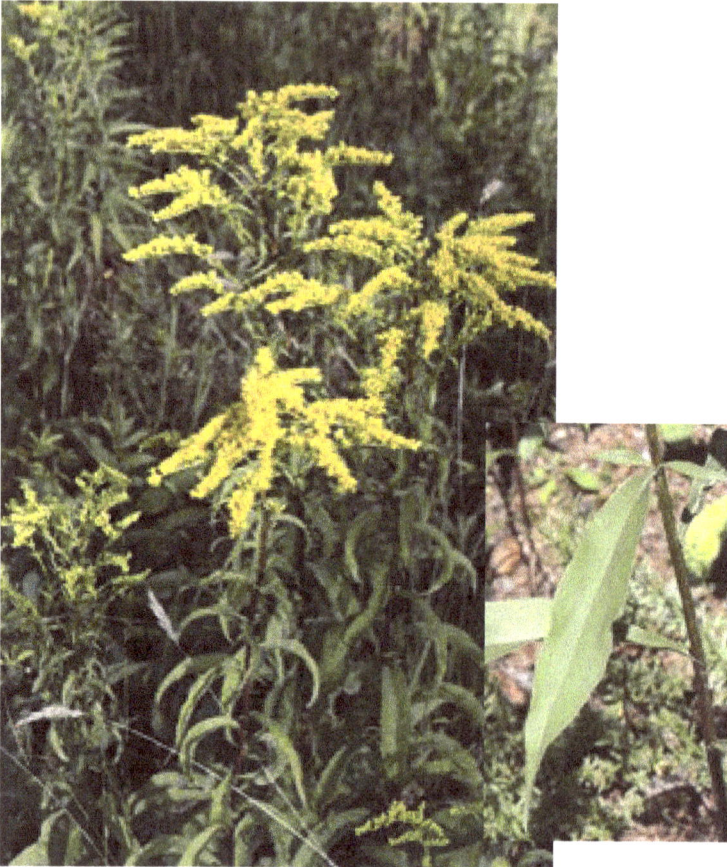

Canada Goldenrod
Solidago canadensis

Family: ASTERACEAE

Canada goldenrod is found in fields and usually grows 2 to 4 feet tall. Along with wrinkled-leaved goldenrod, this is the most common goldenrod on the islands. The flowers are tiny, about 1/8 inch across, and are formed in clusters on upwardly curving stalks. The leaves are lance-shaped, 2 to 6 inches long, and have three veins running the length of the leaf.

Native to the U.S. and Canada, this goldenrod has been introduced into Europe and Asia, where it can be a problematic invasive. With all the invasive plants we have gotten from Europe and Asia, it is interesting to know we have given one back.

July/August-Yellow

Wrinkled-leaved Goldenrod
Solidago rugosa

Family: ASTERACEAE

Wrinkled-leaved goldenrod grows in fields to a height of 2 to 4 feet. Each stalk terminates in clusters, often branched clusters, of tiny yellow flowers. From a distance, wrinkled-leaved and Canada goldenrods look similar but are distinguished by their leaves. Those of wrinkled-leaved goldenrod are broader, have a rougher surface, and lack the three distinct leaf veins seen in Canada goldenrod.

Hawks-Beard
Crepis capillaris

Family: ASTERACEAE

Hawks-beard grows in lawns and fields. The flowers resemble dandelion flowers, but the leaves are distinctive. The plant is from 6 inches to 2 feet tall, with erect branched flower stalks, which terminate in a flower head about 1 inch across. There is a rosette of leaves at the base of the plant. The leaves are from 2 to 8 inches long (depending on the size of the plant), and strap-like with many deep lobes.

July/August-Yellow

Field Sow-Thistle
Sonchus arvensis

Family: ASTERACEAE

This thistle is 2 to 5 feet tall and is found in fields, roadsides, and disturbed areas. Its flower heads are 1 to 2 inches wide. The leaves are lance-shaped, with pointed lobes and prickles, and the leaf bases clasp the stem.

Introduced from Europe, field sow-thistle can be an invasive.

Canada Hawkweed
Hieracium kalmii

Family: ASTERACEAE

Canada hawkweed grows 2 to 4 feet tall and, unlike our other hawk-weeds, it has leaves along the length of its stem, not just at the base. The stalk is branched near its tip, and forms several yellow flower heads, each about 1 inch across. The leaves are 1 to 3 inches long (depending on the size of the plant) and are arrowhead-shaped with toothed margins.
6

July/August-Yellow

Pineapple-weed, Wild Chamomile
Matricaria discoidea

Family: ASTERACEAE

Pineapple-weed grows in disturbed sites like driveways -- look for it at Chebeague's Transfer Station! The plant is 6 to 12 inches tall, with a tightly packed head of tiny yellow flowers. Its leaves are divided into many tiny needle-like points.

Pineapple-weed has been used as an herbal medicine and an herbal tea.

Jewelweed, Spotted Touch-Me-Not
Impatiens capensis

Family: BALSAMINACEAE

2 to 4 feet tall, jewelweed grows in partly shaded wet areas -- roadside ditches, swampy areas, and along streams.   The flowers are 1 to 1½ inches long, conical, and orange with red dots, particularly on the lips of the lower petals. The back end of the flower terminates in a nectar horn, which fills with nectar as a lure for their pollinators (bees and humming-birds).   The leaves are ovate, 2 to 4 inches long, and have toothed margins. The stems are partially translucent.

Juice from jewelweed was used by Native Americans to treat rashes including poison ivy. The name touch-me-not refers to the way its seeds are dispersed. When the mature fruits are brushed against they explode, sending out the seeds.

Fireweed
Chamerion angustifolium

Family: ONAGRACEAE

Fireweed is found in fields and clearings; the plant is a colonizing species following fires (hence its name). Fireweed is 2 to 5 feet tall, with a terminal spike of flowers. The individual flowers are 1 inch across, and have the stamens and stigma exposed. The lance-shaped leaves are 2 to 6 inches long.

Purple Loosestrife
Lythrum salicaria

Family: LYTHRACEAE

Purple loosestrife is 3 to 5 feet tall, with spikes of red/purple flowers, each about 1 inch long. The leaves are lance-shaped and opposite, up to 4 inches long, and the stems are square.

Although attractive, this plant is Eurasian in origin and is considered an invasive in North America. It grows in wet ditches, and marshy areas, and can crowd out other species. In spite of its common name, it is completely unrelated to yellow loosestrife and whorled loosestrife – watch out for those common names!

95

Purple-Leaved Willow-Herb
Epilobium coloratum

Family: ONAGRACEAE

This bushy plant is 2 to 4 feet tall, and grows in marshy areas. The flow-ering stalks form in the axils of the leaves, and each stalk terminates in a ½ inch-long flower with 4 pink petals. The lance-shaped leaves are 2 to 4 inches long, ½ to ¾ inch wide, and toothed.

Smartweed
Persicaria pensylvanica

Family: POLYGONACEAE

Smartweed grows in wet fields and roadsides to a height of 2 to 3 feet. It has spikes of tiny pinkish, white flowers; each flower about 1/8-inch long. The leaves are lance-shaped, with no teeth, and are 4 to 5 inches long and ½ inch wide. Like other members of the Polygonaceae (joint-stem family), the stems bend at each node, as if jointed. Two other members of this family are tearthumb and Japanese knotweed.

July/August-Red/Pink

Maiden Pink
Dianthus deltoides

Family: CARYOPHYLLACEAE

Maiden pink grows about 1 foot tall with flowers ¾ of an inch across. The leaves are linear and 1 to 2 inches long. It likes open and somewhat dry fields.

Native to Europe and introduced into North America, maiden pink is grown horticulturally and may be present in wildflower seed mixes. This photo was taken in the field below the old Thompson house on Chebeague's Littlefield Road; the plant may have been deliberately seeded there.

Deptford Pink
Dianthus armeria

Family: CARYOPHYLLACEAE

Deptford pink grows in fields to a height of about 2 feet. It has a branched upright stem, and forms wonderful pink and white spotted flowers, about ½ inch across.   The leaves are thin, needle-like, and 1 to 2 inches long.

This photo was taken on Jewell Island in the field below the gun emplacements.

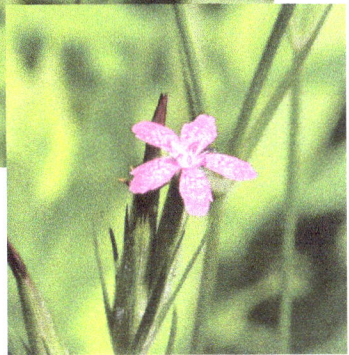

99

July/August-Red/Pink

Beach Rose, Wrinkled Rose
Rosa rugosa

Family: ROSACEAE

Growing to a height of 3 to 5 feet, this rose is often found along the shore because it is salt tolerant, but it can grow in fields and roadsides, and it is grown ornamentally. The flowers are about 3 inches across, with deep red petals, although there is also a white flowered variety. The leaves are 5 to 6 inches long, each with 5 to 9 leaflets. The leaves are wrinkled (rugosa means wrinkled), and the stems are densely covered with prickles. After flowering, the base of the flower develops into a distinctive rose hip, which eventually turns red (it's still green in the photo here). Each rose hip bears 5 long green bracts, another characteristic of this species.

The mature hips are edible and are traditionally used to make jam.

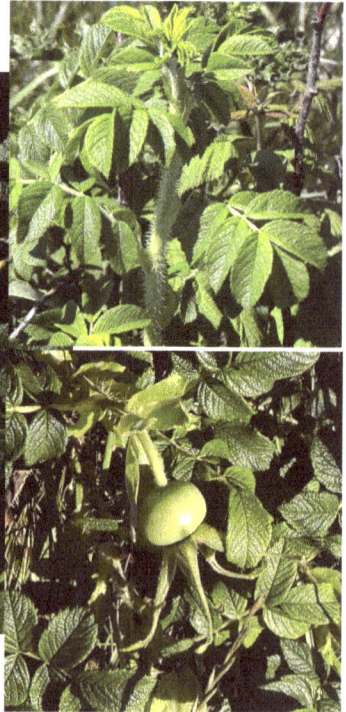

Smooth Rose
Rosa blanda

Family: ROSACEAE

This rose is a low, trailing shrub, up to 3 feet tall, and is found in rocky dry edges of fields and roadways. The leaves are smooth on the top surface, and have tiny hairs on the lower surface that makes that side of the leaf look a little silvery. The stems have thorns mostly only at the leaf bases and branch points (nodes), and the thorns are about ¼-inch long and curve downward. The flowers are pink and about 2 inches across. The hips are small (¼ inch wide) and smooth. My botanical key identifies this as *Rosa blanda*, but the plants on Chebeague have more thorns than are described for *R. blanda*. Apparently, *R. blanda* can hybridize with other rose species; so what we have may be a hybrid with wrinkled rose.

101

July/August–Blue/Purple

Blue Toadflax
Nuttallanthus canadensis

Family: PLANTAGINACEAE

Blue toadflax is easy to overlook, but its tiny flowers are quite pretty. Growing in dry fields and waste sites, it has a slender stalk 1 to 2 feet tall, which terminates in a cluster of ½-inch-diameter blue flowers. Each flower has 3 lobes on the lower petal and two lobes on the upper one. The leaves are narrow and linear, ½ to 1 inch long.

Blue Vervain
Verbena hastata

Family: VERBENACEAE

Blue vervain grows in marshy, damp areas, to a height of 3 to 5 feet. The purple flowers, each about 1/8 inch across, are formed in whorls on spikes at the top of the plant. The flowers mature progressively from the base to the tip of the spike; as one whorl fades the whorl of flowers immediately above them open. Blue vervain's leaves are opposite, lance shaped, toothed, and 2 to 6 inches long.

Heal-All
Prunella vulgaris

Family: LAMIACEAE

Heal-all grows in moist fields and roadsides, and is usually 4 to 12 inches tall.   The stalks terminate in a cluster of blue flowers, ½- to ¾-inch-wide, each of which has an upper petal covering the flower and a lower petal that is fringed (bearded).   The leaves are opposite, lance-shaped, and 3 to 4 inches long.   Young plants are edible in salads or cooked.

Marsh skullcap
Scutellaria galericulata

Family: LAMIACEAE

Marsh skullcap grows in wet, marshy areas, to a height of 15 to 20 inches. The flowers are blue, about 1 inch long, and are formed in pairs in the axils of the leaves. Each flower has a hood-like upper petal and a pro-truding lower petal. The leaves are 1 to 2 inches long, opposite, and ar-rowhead-shaped.

Sea Rocket
Cakile edentula

Family: BRASSICACEAE

Sea rocket is found on the upper end of rocky beaches. It is a salt-tolerant succulent plant 12 to 16 inches tall, with many branched stems, and strap-like leaves about 2 inches long. The tiny flowers each have four pale blue, or sometimes, white petals. Also shown in the photo are the fruits, which are characteristic and easily identifiable.

Bellflower, Harebell
Campanula rapunculoides

Family: CAMPANULACEAE

Growing in fields and roadsides, bellflower has a spike of bell-shaped, pendulous, purple flowers 1 to 1½ inches long. The lower leaves are heart-shaped and 3 to 4 inches long.

The plant would make an attractive ornamental, but it is native to Eurasia and acts as an aggressive invasive in North America, spreading by means of underground stems.

July/August–Blue/Purple

Bittersweet Nightshade, Climbing Nightshade
Solanum dulcamara

Family: SOLANACEAE

This nightshade grows in clearings, along roadsides, and in fields. It is shrubby to viney and can be 3 to 5 feet tall if given the chance. It produces clusters of purple, ½-inch-long, flowers with 5 petals. As the flowers age, the petals curl back exposing the bright yellow stamens. The leaves are 2 to 3 inches long, and larger leaves have lobes at the base. The fruits are initially green, but ripen to red, and are toxic to mammals but apparently not to birds.

The plant in the photo has been pulled back to expose the flowers, so you are seeing the undersides of the leaves.

Blazing Star, Dense Blazing Star
Liatris spicata

Family: ASTERACEAE

Blazing star prefers moist fields and grows to a height of 3 or more feet. It has a dense clump of long, thin, grass-like or lily-like leaves, and sends up several spikes of densely packed flowers, with purple petals.

This plant is a popular ornamental, and where found on the islands, it may be the result of the deliberate spreading of wildflower seeds.

July/August–Blue/Purple

Chicory
Cichorium intybus

Family: ASTERACEAE

Chicory grows in dry fields and roadsides. The plant is 2 to 4 feet tall, and highly branched, with numerous flower heads 1½ inches across. The lower leaves are 3 to 8 inches long and lance-shaped; the upper leaves are smaller.

Chicory is another European import. Its root has been used as a coffee substitute, and the leaves are eaten in salads. Cultivated forms of chicory are radicchio and Belgian endive.

Bull Thistle, Common Thistle
Cirsium vulgare

Family: ASTERACEAE

Bull thistle grows to be 5 to 6 feet high, is highly branched, and has deeply lobed, lance-shaped leaves tipped with long spines. The flowers are 1 to 2 inches across, and have a large, inflated, spiny base. Bull thistle is a biennial plant. In the first year, it grows close to the ground, with a cluster of large spiny leaves that may be 1½ feet long. In the second year, the stem shoots upward, and forms flowers.

The flowers are a favorite of bees and butterflies, and the seeds attract goldfinches.

Canada Thistle, Creeping Thistle
Cirsium arvense

Family: ASTERACEAE

Found in fields and thickets, this plant is a European import and an invasive. It grows to about 3 to 5 feet tall, is highly branched, and has flower
heads that are less than 1 inch across. The leaves are crinkly with spine-
tipped lobes. Lower leaves can be more than 6 inches long; upper leaves
are shorter. Canada thistle spreads by underground stems, which make
it difficult to get rid of once it is established.

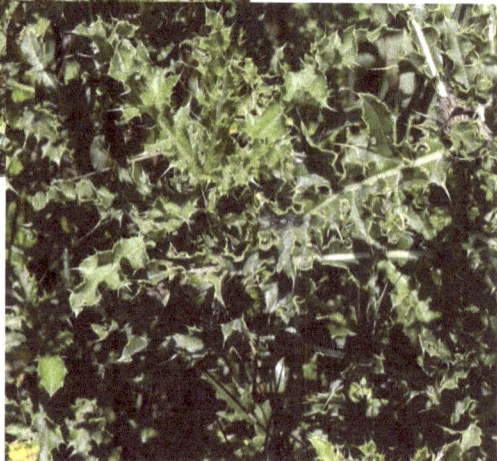

Blue Lettuce, Tall Blue Lettuce
Lactuca biennis

Family: ASTERACEAE

This is a large plant, 6 to 12 feet tall. The leaves are up to 1 foot long, deeply lobed, and with coarse teeth. The flowers are formed in a many-branched cluster at the top of the plant, and each flower is about ½ inch across with light blue petals. Since blue lettuce is in the aster family, each flower is actually a collection of tiny individual flowers. The plant in these photos has nearly finished flowering and is beginning to set seeds.

113

July/August-Green/Brown

Curly Dock
Rumex crispus

Family: POLYGONACEAE

This is the largest of our dock/sorrel species, and can be found in disturbed sites along roadsides, and in fields. The plant has long, branching, flowering stalks up to 3 to 4 feet tall that are densely covered with tiny greenish flowers, which turn red/brown as they age. The leaves are long and narrow, lance-shaped, 4 to 6 inches long, and found mostly at the base of the plant. The plant in this photo is senescing; the leaves have turned from green to red/brown.

The leaves of young dock and sorrel plants (all members of the genus *Rumex*) are edible but somewhat sour due to the presence of oxalic acid.

Common Plantain
Plantago major

Family: PLANTAGINACEAE

This is another plant that likes disturbed sites. It is often found in drive-ways, walkways, and along roadsides. The leaves are 2 to 6 inches long, somewhat ovate to heart shaped. The tiny flowers are formed on spikes 5 to 15 inches tall.

The leaves of young plants can be added to salads. Tinctures prepared from the leaves have a long history of use in herbal medicine for the promotion of wound healing.

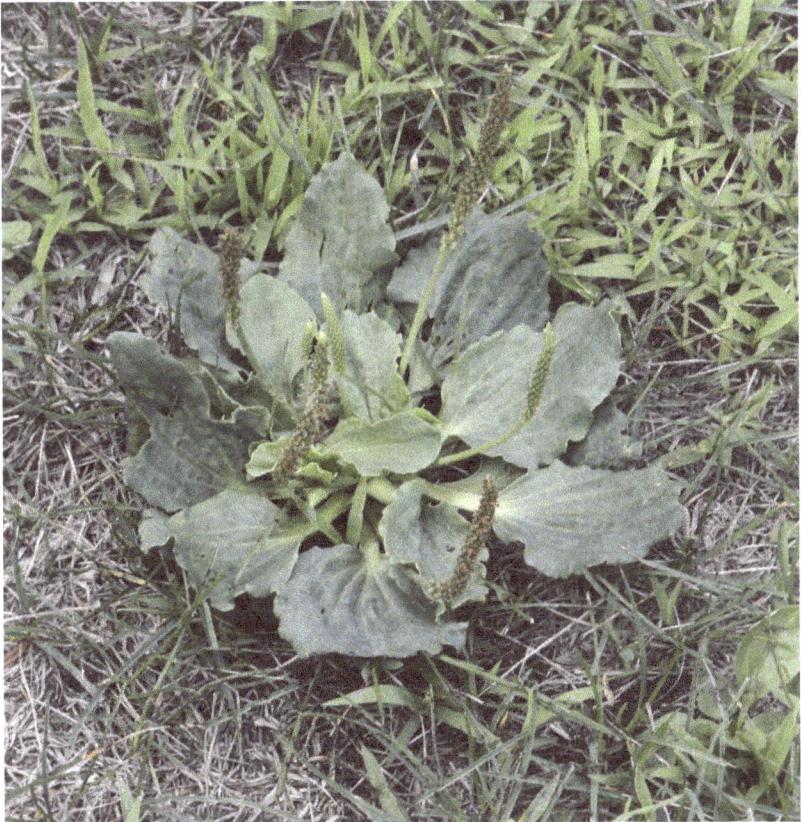

Ragweed, Common Ragweed
Ambrosia artemisiifolia

Family: ASTERACEAE

Ragweed grows in disturbed sites: roadsides, ditches, and construction sites. The plant may be from 1 to 5 feet tall. Its tiny greenish flowers, 1/8-inch long, are formed on spikes, 2 to 4 inches long. The leaves, 2 to 5 inches long, are deeply divided and lobed.

Ragweed pollen is a major source of summer hay fever. The plant is a North American native that has now been spread world-wide. Ambrosia is of Greek origin and means immortal; in Greek mythology ambrosia was the fruit of the gods. So why was ragweed given the scientific genus name Ambrosia? No one seems to know. Carl Linnaeus named this plant from a specimen sent to him from North America. Presumably he knew nothing of its weediness or allergy-inducing properties and decided to give it a fancy name.

Broad-Leaved Cattail
Typha latifolia

Family: TYPHACEAE

Cattail is a marsh plant and grows to 6 or more feet in height. This species has long narrow leaves, and forms its flowers on separate shoots – the characteristic cattail. The individual flowers are very tiny and are bunched together. There are actually separate male and female flowers on this plant. The thick, dark brown, part of the cattail are the female flowers. Above them, the thinner, tan structure contains the male flowers.

The underground stems of this plant were a food source for Native Americans.

Male Flowers

Female Flowers

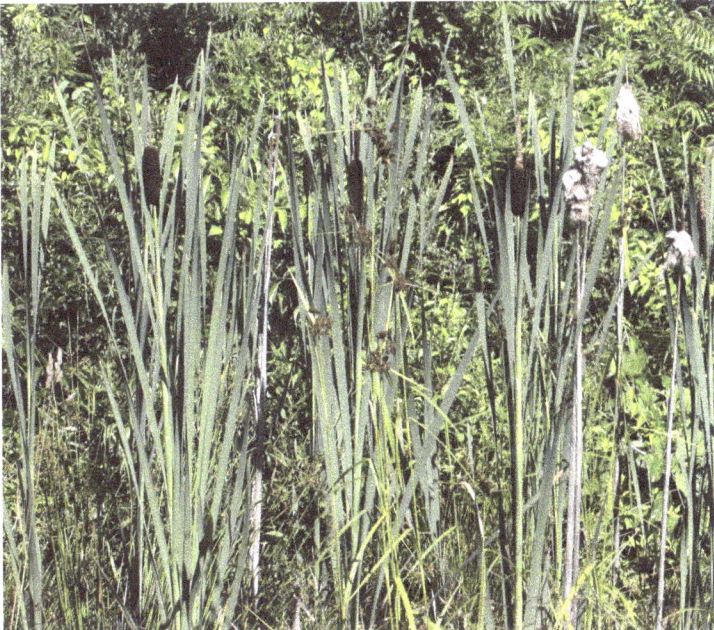

117

September/October-White

In late August and early September the transition to fall begins. Canada and wrinkled-leaved goldenrods continue, Queen Anne's lace is present but declining, and some black-eyed Susans are still around. But in September, and on into October, the asters and new goldenrods predominate. I have identified ten different asters and four goldenrods, but there may be more species of both.

White Goldenrod, Silverrod
Solidago bicolor

Family: ASTERACEAE

White goldenrod likes drier sites in fields, woodland edges, and roadsides. Growing up to 3 feet tall, it has clusters of tiny, ¼-inch-diameter, white flowers. The lance-shaped leaves are 1 to 4 inches long.

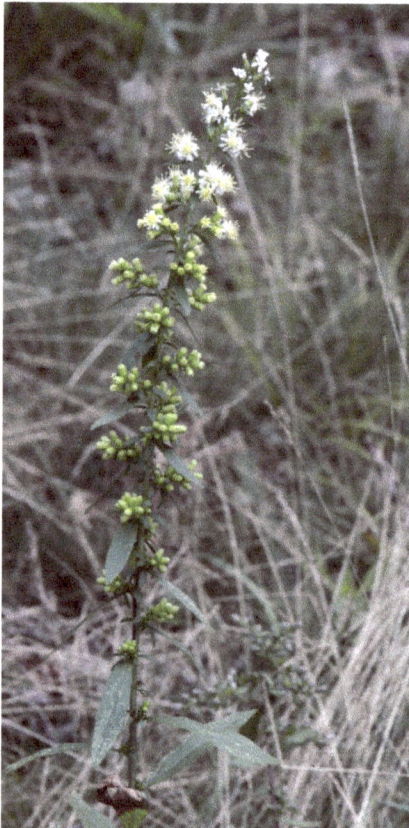

Tall-White Aster, Flat-Topped Aster
Doellingeria umbellata

Family: ASTERACEAE

This aster grows in fields and along roadsides, to a height of 2 to 6 feet. The flowers are about 1 inch in diameter, with a dozen white petals (ray flowers), and are clustered at the top of the plant. The lance-shaped leaves are 2 to 5 inches long and lack petioles.

September/October-White

Calico Aster
Symphyotrichum lateriflorum

Family: ASTERACEAE

Calico aster is found in fields and roadsides. It can be 4 feet tall, but usually is 1 to 2 feet in height. The plant is highly branched, and has clusters of small white flowers (½ inch across) on the branches. Each flower has 12 to 16 white petals (ray flowers), and yellow centers (disc flowers) that turn purple as they age. The leaves are narrow, lance-shaped, lack petioles, and are not toothed. Lower leaves may be 2 to 3 inches long; the upper leaves are usually less than 1 inch in length. The stems may be purple or green.

Whorled Wood Aster
Oclemena acuminata

Family: ASTERACEAE

This aster is a woodland plant growing at the forest edge. It is 8 to 15 inches tall and has a small number of flower heads that are 1 to 1½ inches across. The leaves are up to 6 inches long, are broadly lance-shaped, and have toothed margins. The leaves appear to be in a whorled arrangement but, on close inspection, are actually alternate.

This photo was taken in the wooded area along Roy Hill Road on Chebeague.

September/October-White

Lance-Leaved Aster, Panicled Aster
Symphyotrichum lanceolatum

Family: ASTERACEAE

This aster generally grows in moist fields and roadside ditches. It is usually 2 to 4 feet tall, but can be taller. The plant is highly branched, and the branches end in clusters of 1-inch-wide white flowers (yellow centers), with each flower having 20 to 30 white petals (ray flowers). The leaves are narrow, lack petioles, and are lance-shaped. They are from 1 to 6 inches long, but generally are six times longer than they are wide.

White Wood-Aster
Eurybia divaricata

Family: ASTERACEAE

This aster is from 1 to 3 feet tall, and grows in shaded, wooded areas. The flowers are 1 to 1½ inches across, with 10 to 12 thin, droopy, white petals (ray flowers) that remind me of the petals of the tall white aster. The leaves are broad with sharp-toothed margins. The lower leaves may be heart-shaped with petioles, the upper leaves are broadly lance-shaped and lack petioles.

September/October-White

Pearly Everlasting
Anaphalis margaritacea

Family: ASTERACEAE

Pearly everlasting grows in dry fields and roadsides. It is about 1 foot tall, with clusters of white flower heads, each ¼ inch across with a dark center. The leaves are needle like and 1 to 3 inches long. The entire plant is covered with fine hairs, which give it a silvery look.

Pilewort
Erechtites hieraciifolius

Family: ASTERACEAE

Pilewort is from 1 to 5 feet tall and grows in disturbed sites: roadsides and clearings. The flowers are ½ inch across and 1½ to 2 inches long, with white petals. The flowers never fully open and are surrounded by green bracts. The leaves are 2 to 6 inches long, lance-shaped, and deeply toothed.

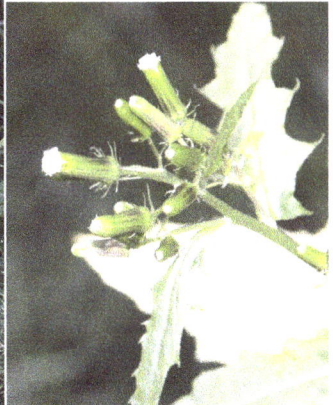

September/October-White

Northern Bugleweed
Lycopus uniflorus

Family: LAMIACEAE

Northern bugleweed is 1 to 3 feet tall and grows in marshy areas. Its flowers are in tight clusters at each node. Each flower is about 1/8-inch long, with 5 lobed, white petals. The leaves are 1 to 3 inches long, lance-shaped, and toothed.

Square stems and opposite leaves, with small flowers forming in the axils of the leaves, are the hallmarks of members of the mint family – the Lamiaceae.

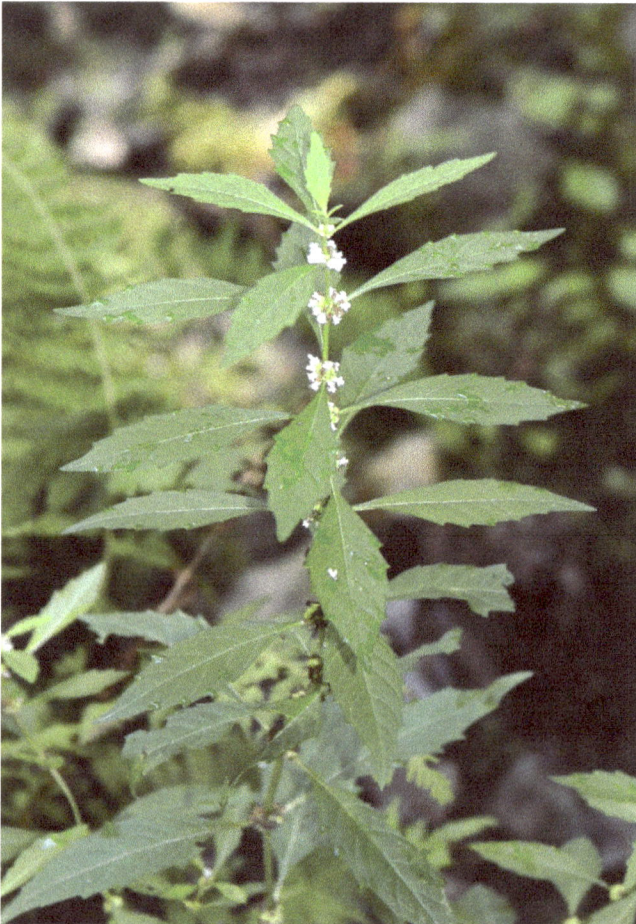

Eyebright
Euphrasia nemorosa

Family: OROBANCHACEAE

This cute little plant is easy to overlook but worth noticing. It is 5 to 10 inches tall and grows in fields. The flowers are ¼ inch across, with lobed white petals, that have yellow markings and blue stripes at the center of the lower petals. The leaves are no more than ½-inch long with toothed margins. The stems are purple, hairy, and branched.

Eyebright was used in traditional western herbal medicine to treat eye inflammation. Like all members of the family Orobanchaceae, eyebright is semiparasitic, tapping into the roots of other plants for some of its nutrition.

Japanese Knotweed
Fallopia japonica

Family: POLYGONACEAE

In September, this shrub forms sprays of attractive white flowers, about ¼ inch across. But don't be fooled by the pretty flowers; this plant is one of our most troublesome invasives. Japanese knotweed grows in thickets 5 to 10 feet tall. It has oval, almost heart-shaped leaves, 3 to 6 inches long.

Many islanders call this plant "bamboo", which it resembles because of its jointed and hollow stems, and its habit of spreading by underground runners. However, bamboo is in the grass family and Japanese knotweed is in the joint-stem family – the Polygonaceae. Japanese knotweed is very difficult to eradicate; it quickly regrows after mowing, and is hard to dig up without heavy equipment.

Nodding Ladies'-Tresses
Spiranthes cernua

Family: ORCHIDACEAE

This sweet little orchid grows in fields to a height of 10 to 15 inches. The flower stalk bears 15 to 20 tiny, ½-inch-long, white flowers, that are arranged in a spiral around the stalk. The leaves are grass-like and about half the length of the flower stalk. Do you see the bee in action, pollinating?

September/October-Yellow

Grass-Leaved Goldenrod
Euthamia (Solidago) graminifolia

Family: ASTERACEAE

Grass-leaved goldenrod grows in fields and roadsides, often mixed in with Canada goldenrod. It is 2 to 4 feet tall, and has spreading branches about halfway up the stem, which terminate in clusters of yellow flowers that are a bit larger than those of Canada goldenrod. The leaves are narrow, 1 to 5 inches long, and have only a single vein visible, the midrib.

Downy Goldenrod
Solidago puberula

Family: ASTERACEAE

Downy goldenrod grows in fields and roadsides, but seems to prefer drier sites than the Canada and grass-leaved goldenrods. It is up to 3 feet tall, with an erect stem terminating in a spike of tiny yellow flowers. The leaves are lance-shaped, up to 5 inches long, and, like the grass-leaved golden-rod, have only a distinct midrib without obvious lateral veins. The stem is often red and is covered with fine hairs.

September/October-Yellow

Seaside Goldenrod
Solidago sempervirens

Family: ASTERACEAE

Seaside goldenrod grows in dunes and marshy areas by the shore. It is salt-tolerant and has thick strap-like fleshy leaves compared with our other goldenrods. It is generally 2 to 4 feet tall, and the lower leaves may be over a foot long.

Devil's Beggar-Ticks
Bidens frondosa

Family: ASTERACECE

This species flowers in late summer and early fall, and is easy to over-look because its flower heads have few to no petals (ray flowers). The plant is up to 2 feet tall, with deeply divided leaves (pinnate leaves). The leaflets are several inches long, lance-shaped, and their margins are distinctly toothed. The stems are reddish brown, branched, and the branches terminate in yellow to orange-brown flower heads that are less than 1 inch across. At the base of each flower head are 6 to 8 leaf-like appendages (bracts). Devil's beggar-ticks is found in wet fields or wet ditches.

September/October-Yellow

Butter-And-Eggs, Yellow Toad Flax
Linaria vulgaris

Family: PLANTAGINACEAE

Butter-and-eggs grows in dry fields; this photo was taken in the parking area of the Rose's Point shore access on Chebeague. The plant is 1 to 2 feet tall, with very narrow leaves, and is tipped with clusters of yellow and orange flowers. The flowers are about 1 inch long and have long nectar horns at their backs. The nectar horns are where sugars accumulate as a reward for pollinators, in this case probably butterflies and bees.

Small-Flowered Agalinis, Smallflower False Foxglove
Agalinis paupercula

Family: OROBANCHACEAE

This small plant grows in wet fields to a height of 6 to 10 inches. The vase-shaped pink/purple flowers are about ½ inch long with five lobes. The leaves are awl-shaped and 1 to 1½ inches long. Like eyebright, this plant is a semiparasite, getting some of its nutrients from the roots of surrounding plants.

New York Aster
Symphyotrichum novi-belgii

Family: ASTERACEAE

This is one of our most common asters. It has pale blue petals, and lance-shaped leaves that clasp the stem (no petioles present). The plant grows in fields and roadsides, and is 2 to 4 feet tall. The flower heads are 1 to 1½ inches across, and have 25 to 50 petals (ray flowers). The New York aster and the New England aster seem similar in description but are easily distinguished. The flowers of the New England aster are bright purple, there are 50 to 75 petals on each flower, and the leaves are much more crowded together than on the New York aster.

New England Aster
Symphyotrichum novae-angliae

Family: ASTERACEAE

The New England aster grows in fields and roadsides to a height of 2 to 4 feet. Its flowers have bright blue/purple petals, and each flower head has 50+ petals (ray flowers). This species is not common on Chebeague, and the ones that are present may in fact have escaped from cultivation. New England aster is a popular ornamental plant.

September/October-Blue/Purple

Blue-Wood Aster, Heart-Leaved Aster
Symphotrichum cordifolium

Family: ASTERACEAE

Growing at woodland edges to a height of 1 to 3 feet, this aster has heart-shaped lower leaves with distinct petioles. The flowers are ¾ to 1 inch across with pale blue/purple petals (ray flowers). On some plants the petals can be so pale they are almost white. Each flower has 10 to 15 petals.

Large-Leaved Aster
Eurybia macrophylla

Family: ASTERACEAE

This shade-loving aster grows in wooded sites, to a height of 1 to 4 feet, and has the largest leaves of any of our asters. The flowers have 10 to 15 pale blue petals (ray flowers). The lower leaves are heart-shaped, 4 to 12 inches long, and have long petioles. The upper leaves on the flower stalks are smaller and often lack petioles.

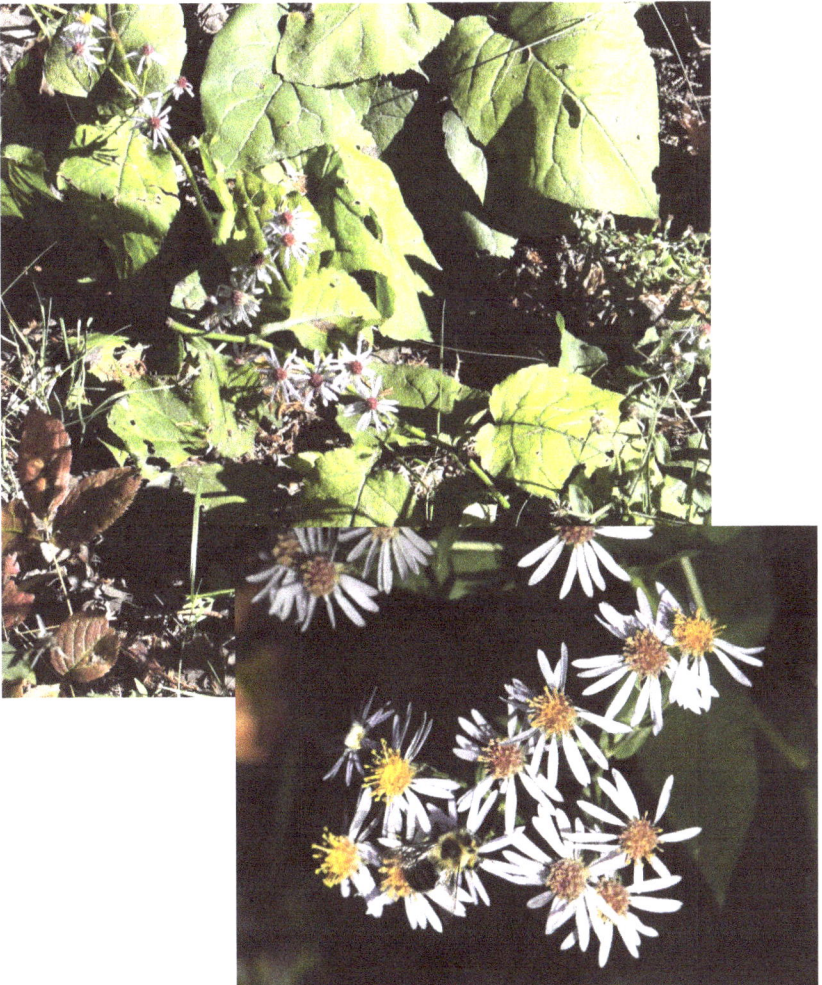

Stiff-Leaved Aster
Ionactis linariifolia

Family: ASTERACEAE

This low-growing aster (usually only 6 to 8 inches tall) is very common in September and October. It has 1-inch-long, needle-like leaves, and grows in woodland edges and dry fields. The blue/purple flowers are about 1 inch across.

Beech-drops
Epifagus virginiana

Family: OROBANCHACEAE

This woodland plant is a root parasite and grows on the roots of beech trees. It lacks chlorophyll and has scale-like leaves. The flowers are reddish brown and ½ inch long. I have seen this under the beech trees on Roy Hill Road near Second Wind Farm on Chebeague, but look for it in the early fall anywhere there are beech trees.

141

INDEX

www.ingramcontent.com/pod-product-compliance
Lightning Source LLC
Chambersburg PA
CBHW050844270326
41930CB00020B/3463